A Circle of Light

Transform Grief into a
Unique Opportunity
for Guidance

A Circle
of Light

Transform Grief into a
Unique Opportunity
for Guidance

Adele Vincent

Winchester, UK
Washington, USA

First published by Sixth Books, 2013
Sixth Books is an imprint of John Hunt Publishing Ltd., Laurel House, Station Approach,
Alresford, Hants, SO24 9JH, UK
office1@jhpbooks.net
www.johnhuntpublishing.com
www.6th-books.com

For distributor details and how to order please visit the 'Ordering' section on our website.

Text copyright: Adele Vincent 2012

ISBN: 978 1 78099 768 1

A CIP catalogue record for this book is available from the British Library.

Scripture quotations are taken from the New American Standard Bible Copyright © 1960, 1962, 1963, 1968, 1971, 1972, 1973, 1975, 1977, 1995 by The Lockman Foundation.

Design: Stuart Davies

Printed and bound by CPI Group (UK) Ltd, Croydon, CR0 4YY

We operate a distinctive and ethical publishing philosophy in all areas of our business, from our global network of authors to production and worldwide distribution.

CONTENTS

'Stranger than truth.'
For my mother, Jeanne
Thank you for your love and wisdom, and for teaching me
anything is possible

Acknowledgments

To my father: I would be lost without you.

To my husband and other half: I couldn't have done it without you. Words cannot express my gratitude for your loving support and belief in me.

To my dancing son: your smile is the reason I exist. Thank you for being you.

To my mother-in-law, my second mother: you taught me how to love and the importance of family. I owe so much to you.

To my father-in-law: *grazie* for showing me how beautiful Italy is (even when you were violently ill). You taught me how to embody passion, even in silence.

To Jean, my second grandmother: you made me love books and Georgia languid afternoons. I will always miss you.

To my family in France: I'm so proud to have family as caring and warm as you.

To my family in America: I hope this is a proud testament to our family. I am waiting to read the next generation's record, M.M.

To Nona Maria: you are a legend. *Need I say more?*

To Andrea: for being the best Zio ever!

To Rebecca: you are the sister I never had. You taught me how to fight for the things that matter.

To my wonderful friends: thank you for listening to me. Your friendship has seen me through hard times.

To W. Family: for showing me Never Never Land really does exist and how to fly.

To the members of Ask Angel: you changed my life and made me rethink what it means to be spiritual. Thank you so much.

To L.F.: 'Thanks' just isn't enough. You launched me.

To my patient, long-enduring English teachers, Mrs. Jetmore and J. Zaccara; and to the many math tutors I had over the years:

I've not forgotten you, because you are forever a part of my life.

Most of all, this book would not have been realized without the hard work of 6th Books and Barbara, my publisher: thank you for being lovely, bubbly and taking a chance on me.

To the wonderful staff and brains behind John Hunt: if only all publishers and imprints could be like you.

Dear Readers,

I trust you will use prudence and safety in following the 11 steps of this book. The techniques, tools and exercises cited in this book are not a substitute for medical or psychological treatment. Grief is a very delicate emotion which has the potential to overwhelm us, especially after a traumatic event. This is why professional help is so important after experiencing traumatic loss.

This book is an account of my personal journey with grief. However, I hope you will find solace and gentle support in this work. Most of all, I hope I can encourage healing and turn the grief you may be experiencing into a unique opportunity for guidance. Losing a loved one is never easy. None of us has the answer alone, but together we can find answers.

Today, we begin a journey to understand the true nature of grief and how death can be an uplifting experience, positively marking our spiritual and physical lives.

Light & Love,

Adele Vincent

Author Notes

There are so many books out there about bereavement. Go to any bookstore and the shelves are packed with books and memoirs on the subject. One of the reasons I chose to write this book is that I believe people can relate to my story. I know what it feels like to lose your mother at a young age, your aunt, grandmother or brother. I lost a lot of special people in my life, but I remained resilient through these losses, focusing on the transformative nature of death.

Yes, death can be uplifting. You may find this impossible to believe, but just like birth it can bring us closer to the divine. My book guides readers through a divine journey. This journey consists of 11 steps to transform grief into guidance. We often lose sight of goals or our true purpose when we experience big changes like death, job loss or the birth of a child. *A Circle of Light* gives readers the tools and techniques to confront life's challenges and the doubt each of us experiences.

After losing my mother, I wanted to read something uplifting, something to see me through the days after her death. I didn't find the perfect self-help book. Everyone is different. In my case I wanted a concrete but practical guide to the afterlife. I don't think such a book exists, simply because we haven't found the answers. I hope this will change as people grow more open to the subject. I decided to share my own experiences, not only to uplift others, but also to start a dialogue. My wish is that this book will change people's views on life after death and encourage them to explore the subject more. This is an account of my journey to become a more spiritual person and how I turned grief into a unique opportunity for guidance.

We are all capable of receiving guidance, if we only open our hearts and eyes to what is right in front of us.

Preface

The Energy Cycle of Life and Death and *The Cycle of Grief*

Changing the Way We Think about Grief

By picking up this book, you show that you are open to grief and its greatest gift: healing. Grief isn't the end. In many ways it's a circle which allows us to look at our choices and gain vital perspective.

Grief taught me many things. It showed me how to appreciate the small things, a loved one's cherished smile and a good friend's sympathetic embrace. Grief deeply enriched my life. I want to share these lessons with you, but most of all I want readers to understand they are on a very special journey to turn grief into guidance.

My journey started long before my mother passed away. Her death was the culmination of many invisible forces in my life. Eight years ago I sat in a windy field listening to endless speeches on Graduation Day. I was lucky enough to have my mother present at the ceremony. Like most 18-year-olds, I was unaware of how quickly life could change and just how unprepared I would be for the changes that would occur in 3 years: mainly my mother's death.

People say ignorance is bliss, but I say youth is bliss. It gives us the precarious illusion of invincibility. While Icarus flew too close to the sun and melted, when we delve into the subject of mortality and the possibility of life after death many of us shut down. This book is not about life and death. It is about something so much more important: spirituality. I passionately believe that spirituality is the only way to turn back the clocks, slow the passage of time and make every second of our lives count.

One quote did remain with me on Graduation Day:

We shall not cease from exploration
And the end of all our exploring
Will be to arrive where we started
And know the place for the first time.
(T.S. Eliot, *Four Quartets*)

This quote guided me during the first days of university, the breathless moment I walked down the aisle with my father, and the dark days following my mother's death. I always draw comfort from the idea that life is a journey which leads us back to our true selves, the soul.

The death of a loved one gives us the opportunity to explore the deeper side of life and many of the questions we avoided asking over the years like, 'Who am I?' 'What do I really want?' 'Why are we here?' These existential questions, while frightening, point to a deep-rooted need within each of us to feel connected to something greater than our physical selves.

The more we understand, the less we fear and, really, that is the overriding message of this book. In 11 steps you will complete your own journey. Each chapter represents an important step in that journey: starting with the first chapter, Learn to Love, and ending with the last chapter, Practice Appreciation. While I often cite my own experiences to illustrate the effectiveness of each step, I have also listed techniques in simple bullet-point form to break down information.

The 11 steps are very simple. The aim of these steps and their accompanying chapters is to transform grief into a positive, life-affirming experience.

1. Learn to Love: *The Spiritual Checklist*
2. Pay Attention to Coincidences: *Techniques to Cleanse Thoughts*
3. Recognize and Interpret Signs: *Common Signs Loved Ones Use*

4. Accept Loss: *How Loss Can Positively Affect Our Lives*
5. Document Your Journey: *Useful Tools*
6. Don't Lose Faith—Ask for Guidance: *Breakthrough Grief*
7. Be Skeptical, But Don't Let Fear Get the Best of You: *Counteract Doubt*
8. The Three 'A's: Attend, Attune and Attain: *Achieve Spiritual Goals*
9. Don't Give Up—It's Never Too Late: *Techniques to Encourage Healing*
10. Trust Your Intuition: *Exercises to Increase Intuition*
11. Practice Appreciation: *The Importance of Mindfulness in Our Lives*

Last, but not least, remember we are all spiritual beings. Spirituality is innate. It cannot be given and it cannot be taken away from you. Spirituality should never be about one person believing he or she holds all the answers. Each of us has a journey to complete, but that journey would mean little without the collective narrative of humankind. Every step we take, even death, brings us closer to the meaning of life.

Circles of Light

Light, as you might guess, is an important theme of the work. Light is closely associated with the process of grief. Grief can be a healing experience, but only if the griever works with the light of the spiritual world, not the dark. In times of grief, many of us may revisit dark emotions of resentment, guilt and anger. This is completely normal and a vital step in the grieving process. While it is important to acknowledge these sentiments and their role in our lives, we should not indulge in these feelings. They can overwhelm us and shadow our choices. This is why light plays such an important role in our spiritual lives. It nourishes the soul and grounds us in our true purpose, deflecting from the darker inclinations of the ego, like fear or hatred. I will explain the difference between the ego and the soul in Step 7: Be Skeptical, But Don't Let Fear Get the Best of You.

Everything we know about the spirit world is based on what we perceive as 'light.' The title of the book refers to two types of light: inner light and outer light. The inner light is the light of the spiritual consciousness, and the outer light is the light of the spiritual beings that guide and protect us. Countless civilizations have depicted winged beings of the unseen world. The notion of angels or spirit guides exists in many faiths.

Light is one way to describe the invisible energy that makes up the spirit world. This energy is eternal or circular in its very nature, much like the light of the aura. Auras are also depicted in many works of art. In the religious works of Italian artists, this light was depicted as a halo. In Eastern works, this light is sometimes manifested as the third eye of spiritual knowledge.

Most people do not see auras or angels, but with practice we can all begin to see the radiant light which surrounds us. Some experts suggest that angels or spirit guides operate at a much higher vibration, which is why we struggle to see them on earth. While we cannot see angels, there are other ways we can recognize their presence and connect with their loving energy. I outline certain techniques in Step 3: Recognize and Interpret Signs.

How Grief Connects Us

There is so much about energy we don't know. While we know energy can neither be created nor destroyed, we don't know what happens to the energy of our body and mind when we die. This is a field of study which is limitless in its potential to explain the mystery of existence and lessen the pain of grief.

Fortunately, the way we think about death as a society is changing. Several books and TV programs have lessened the taboo surrounding death. There are real, verifiable accounts of people who died only to return and tell loved ones of their experience of the afterlife. These accounts suggest that death is not an end but a beginning of another existence, which is why grief shouldn't be thought of as a negative experience, but as a process of transformation.

One way to think of death and birth is to view them as a constant interchange of energy. This interchange resembles two circles or a number '8'. This interchange is as constant as it is infinite.

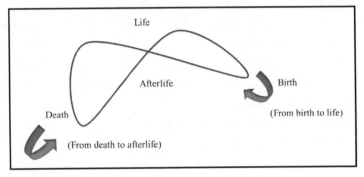

The Energy Cycle of Life & Death: The Journey of the Soul

This 'Cycle of Life' mirrors the 'Cycle of Grief.' Both processes begin with death or loss. The end result of this process is healing or a rebirth of the soul.

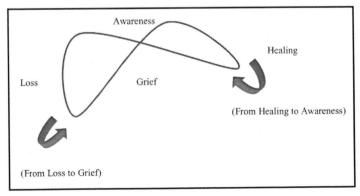

The Cycle of Grief

What similarities do you notice between these cycles? Let us start with the obvious: both cycles are eternal. However, this is not immediately obvious to the griever. Grief is most often experienced in two stages, giving the illusion that the process is finite. For instance, it is normal to experience grief with loss, or healing with awareness, but few of us would associate loss with the end result of the cycle: self-awareness.

We view our lives in broken events. Only a death or birth in our close circle of friends and family can shake us out of this illusion. Our lives are not finite points in time. They are a part of a much greater narrative. Like rivers, we return to the source only to begin the process all over again. Some call this process 'reincarnation.' I think this is too finite a term to describe such a constant and eternal cycle. It is the exchange of energy, the soul's energy.

Many of us view loss and grief as an unpleasant experience which has to be suffered for a period before we can get on with the business of living. Unfortunately, this way of thinking represses one of the most important stages of grief: healing and the spiritual awareness it brings.

Transforming Grief into Guidance

It took me a long time to realize I could do something with the grief I felt for my mother. This was nothing short of an epiphany. I carried around this terrible burden. I liken it to a very large suitcase without wheels. Wherever I went I lugged invisible 'emotional baggage.' Friends and family couldn't see I was weighed down by emotions, but I think somehow they sensed I was suffering. I wasn't myself.

It never occurred to me that the suitcase was useful. If I had paid more attention, I would have realized I was being prepared for a journey. Everything I needed was in the contents of the suitcase. Each of us has an invisible suitcase we carry around with us. At times, its presence is barely noticeable. Other times we feel its weight more acutely. It becomes a burden which we find ourselves constantly thinking about.

What's Inside Your Suitcase?
- Emotions
- Memories
- Unresolved conflict
- Insecurity

While much of this content may seem negative at first glance, the issues represent golden opportunities for healing and growth. Insecurity and unresolved conflict are the pillars of grief. They often keep us from moving on from the loss of a loved one. We find ourselves consumed by feelings of guilt, remorse, anger or hopelessness. Because we can no longer engage in physical discourse with our loved one, we feel their absence all the more.

I often hear people express a simple desire to speak again with a loved one. 'If only I could tell them how I really feel' is a common refrain in many of my discussions. I usually reply, 'You can! I did and you can too.'

What if I told you your loved one was patiently waiting for you to contact them with the help of angels? There is nothing stopping you from making contact, except *you* of course! Sometimes we are our own worst enemy. Disbelief is the skeptic's crutch. People forget that skepticism means to question, not to refute information! I think of myself as a reformed skeptic. I regularly question the information I encounter, but I make a point of researching any questions I have, before making a decision to accept the information as true or false. So feel free to question the information you encounter in this book, but make an effort to be open and complete the 11 steps of your personal journey.

Take a good look at the baggage you are dragging around with you. If you can be honest with yourself, there is no reason you cannot heal and gain new levels of awareness. You might be stuck in the initial phases of loss and grief, too afraid or too bogged down mentally to think of healing. What is holding you back? Do you feel angry?

I did and still do. Healing is a constant process. My relationship with my mother was far from perfect, but it was a loving bond and this was the most important aspect of our relationship—and still is. I learned to forgive her, but most of all I learned to forgive myself. I realized that when we are angry with someone, we are usually angry at ourselves. In my case, I was angry at myself for not demanding more from my mother and myself. I didn't know it at the time, but this anger was a barrier between us. Inadvertently, I prevented her contact.

This is why insecurity and unresolved conflict are the two biggest pillars of grief. If left unresolved, they weigh us down and keep us in the initial stages of grief. As a consequence, our spiritual growth is stunted. Healing and awareness are delayed and we begin to think of death as something unbearably tragic. Death is just one step on the soul's journey. It is neither unbearable nor tragic. It is simply one stage of transformation.

My mother and I could have been so much closer in our limited time together, but our mutual fear of intimacy and trust issues prevented this. Her death represented a turning point in our story. We passed through healing to new levels of awareness. I no longer grieve for my mother. If I feel sad, I know I am grieving for myself and the mistakes I made. Yes, I miss her every day and yes, there are times when nostalgia hits me so hard it feels like a freight train coming fast through the darkness of my mind to knock me down.

It doesn't take much—a favorite song or the way the sun shines on a spring day. On an especially clear day, my mother used to say it was a 'diamond day' made for us to enjoy. Sometimes on clear days I feel sad, but the sadness is passing. It is merely a wish that things might have been different. I don't have deep-seated regrets, because I know I am a much better, stronger and wiser person. I would not be the person I am today without experiencing the loss of my mother. Loss is often the first step towards a greater sense of self-awareness.

Nostalgia is simply a reminder that we are emotional beings. I don't consider myself emotional, but I am glad I experience nostalgia, because it is a reminder that my feelings for my mother are real. I arrived at a happy compromise. I use nostalgia as inspiration, but I never let it weigh me down. My suitcase is purposefully light. I don't allow thoughts or insecurities to fester. Instead, I try to channel my emotional frustrations into productive projects. This is an outlet for any remaining grief. There are many ways to positively honor a person's memory. I discuss several techniques in Step 4: Accept Loss.

I take each day at a time, but I can honestly say that the process of grief has brought me deeper levels of awareness which continue to enrich my life. Grief has made me a better person. It inspired me to share my story with others who have experienced loss. I met so many wonderful people on my journey. More importantly, I learned that loss and grief are essential components of the human story. Without them we would be ships without anchors. They remind us we are mortal and steel our resolve to realize our soul's purpose. I hope this book will be an anchor for readers in a confusing time. Loss uproots us, but if we willingly learn from its lessons we have the unprecedented opportunity to grow and lead more fulfilling lives.

Step 1

Learn to Love: *The Spiritual Checklist*

This is a step I've been working on my whole life. It is the first and most important step to turning grief into guidance. I can't count the number of times I've made a promise to be more loving, only to break it in the heat of the moment with family and friends. Losing a loved one represents a special opportunity to learn to love, not only those around us, but more importantly ourselves.

Today, you begin a journey to understand grief and the importance of guidance in our lives. It might be a familiar journey that you embarked on several times, but feel you haven't quite 'arrived' yet. You wonder why you continue to suffer, if there isn't some important lesson to be learned in the experience of loss. It may be a journey that is very new and strange to you. Whatever your reasons for reading this book, know you are not alone. You are loved by many. Step by step, you will learn to return this love: both visible and invisible. There will be plenty of signs and encouragement along the way. The trick is to pay attention.

Like every good journey we embark on, preparation goes a long way. Here's your personal checklist.

The Spiritual Checklist for Learning to Love
✓ An Inquisitive Mind:
Throw out the rulebook. Admit you know nothing. It may be hard to understand at this moment, as you may be a very cultivated person of impressive status, but accept that everything you know is but a mere fraction of the collective knowledge that exists in the universe.

✓ A Loving Heart:

Open your heart. Learning to love isn't just about learning to love others. It also means loving oneself and life, and appreciating the interconnectedness of everything we experience. People often think of love in compartmentalized terms. We tend to favor certain kinds of love, relishing the early days of a new love affair or the undivided attention of a good friend. These are the kinds of relationships we find easiest to initiate, but what about the unrelenting relative who we can never seem to come to an agreement with or the beggar on the street corner?

✓ Be Willing to Ask the Difficult Questions:

'How do I behave in these situations?' We are all guilty of turning a blind eye. Many of us feel frustration when we encounter people who are radically different from us. We are incensed when someone expresses an extreme view that doesn't tally with our own view. This isn't a lecture. It's a lifelong lesson which we never stop learning.

✓ A Journal:

Take a good look in the mirror. Don't be afraid to meet your own gaze. Be honest, really honest. What do you see? Do you see fear, anger and silence? Maybe you see nothing. That's okay. Take a journal and write your observations daily.

The Journey

Learning to love is about levels of awareness. When you become aware of your behavior, you can change it. We often think of ourselves as loving and open people. However, if we make an honest assessment of our lives, we see there are areas which could be improved or relationships which could be enriched. Self-awareness is something we learn by facing the most difficult tasks in our life, like confronting loss. I learned to truly love when I lost my mother unexpectedly after my 22nd birthday. I realized

I had spent my life escaping difficult situations because I believed I wasn't strong enough.

Every person is different. It took a great loss for me to understand how to love the important people in my life and reconnect with my spirituality. The reasons we choose to reconnect with our spirituality are ours alone. What remains indisputable is our shared need for spirituality. Learning to love is about submitting oneself to an experience like grief and its greatest gift: healing.

Even if your loved one experienced a tragic or untimely death, know that death is simply a process of transformation. There is perspective to be gained from every loss. I speak with authority on this issue, having lost my brother when he was just 2 months old, my mother when I was barely into my twenties and my aunt at 15. My brother's death was one of the most transformative experiences because it taught my family to love in different ways, strengthening our family ties.

How I Began My Journey

The person who embodied love and faith best was my mother. She was a believer in all things spiritual: the redemptive power of love, fate, God and the importance of exercising personal will. She had an unquestioning faith, the kind that permeated every inch of her face, resonating in her startling blue-green eyes. People were afraid of her. I think more often than not they were afraid of the intensity of her beliefs and the fierceness with which she defended her views.

In a society where people were reluctant to speak of their views of the afterlife, she was something of a trailblazer, befriending Raymond Moody, author of the bestselling book, *Life after Life*. They often discussed their ideas about life after death. I think these discussions framed her opinions on the possibility of communication. However, her spirituality was deeply rooted. It was something she inherited from a long line of churchgoing, corset-wearing women.

Mom's passing on Thanksgiving Day 2007 represented a turning point in my life. It taught me to slow down and appreciate the small things in life. We live our lives in such a mad panic. When is the last time you called a loved one to tell them just how much they really mean to you? I wish I had done this more when Mom was alive. It's so easy to get distracted and forget to spend quality time with the people who really count. It's never too late. You may think because you lost someone, they are no longer part of your life. This is not true. The people we love will always be a part of our lives. The memories and lessons they taught us continue to live on with us, helping us heal and grow as people.

The Importance of Angels in Our Lives

Most people believe in angels or spirit guides because they feel they were helped at some crucial moment in their lives. I use the term 'angels' to describe the elevated spiritual beings that surround and protect us. These divine beings assist us in realizing and fulfilling our greater purpose. Each of us has several angels guiding us through our journey. Do not hesitate to call upon them in times of need or doubt. This is their divine purpose.

How Angels Assist Us in Learning to Love

Angels are the embodiment of love and compassion. They can help us access our deepest fears and darkest beliefs, working to change the way we think about the world and our place in it. When miracles happen, an angel is usually close by, ensuring that an outcome is positively realized. However, an angel cannot shape fate or free will. These are two factors which are not open to influence. Angelic beings will guide you, but they will not make important decisions for you. Our lessons are ours alone to learn.

This is why those of us who struggle to love find it difficult to invite angels into our lives. We often find ourselves caught in a vicious circle. We struggle to love and in that struggle we find little room to heal and grow. The loss of a loved one sends us spiraling further down. Fortunately, angels can help us change our patterns of behavior and transform grief into guidance. However, the griever must become more aware of the presence of angels in his life before he can work with them to truly heal.

People often wonder why they have never had an angelic encounter. The answer is simple. You haven't invited the angels into your life! If you do not give them permission to work with you, they will stay behind the scenes. The more you invite them into your life, the more they are able to help. It is very much a give-and-take relationship. Some angels or spirit guides grow by helping people on earth. So remember you aren't the only one on a journey to become more aware of your purpose; angels have missions too!

How You Welcome an Angel into Your Life

• **Research**

Do some homework on the subject of angels. There are many saints and archangels to call upon for help and healing. The more you read, the more informed you will become. Knowledge is power. As a consequence, your mind will be less blocked and more open to their presence. I like to call on Archangel Michael or Mother Mary, but I also like reading about the life of Saint Francis of Assisi. It is a highly personal preference which isn't dependent on religious ties.

➤ **A note on researching**

You aren't restricted to saints or angels; you can also call upon famous people in history. They might not always arrive to help (sprits do not always dedicate their lives to others) but it is worth trying if you are finding it difficult to connect with an angel. I love Saint Francis of Assisi because of his connection with animals and his chosen life of poverty. We share a love of animals. This connection helps me tune in to his presence.

• Pray

It's the most simple of techniques, but it works wonders. A prayer is a silent meditation of intent. The more we ask for help, the more intention we have of receiving that help when it appears in our lives.

➢ A note on praying

If you are struggling with the grieving process, please remember to pray nightly. It is important you focus on intention, because feelings can manifest in our physical lives. If you are feeling ill or poorly, you will soon find yourself down physically. Prayers can help control our waking thoughts and welcome angels into our lives to help heal and uplift us. I often pray to Archangel Michael when I am feeling tired or stressed. I always wake up feeling refreshed and positive the next morning.

• Visualize

Visualizing angels is never an easy task. Even some of the greatest artists of history struggled to conceive how angels look. I have a ceramic painting of Saint Francis that I like to look at in the kitchen. It sounds silly, but taking a few seconds out of my busy day to look at the image helps me to relax and refocus my energies.

➢ A note on visualizing angels

Visiting a religious place, museum or website where you can find pictures of inspirational spiritual figures might also help you relax and refocus throughout the day.

• Other Techniques

You can also say mantras throughout the day like, 'Angels, I welcome you into my life.' If you want to increase the potency of a mantra, leave your bedroom door or office door open. You can even leave notes on your desk, reminding the angels that you invited them into your life. Angels have a sense of humor and will appreciate your invitation at a physical and spiritual level.

How Angels Help Us Connect with Our Loved Ones

It is important to make a distinction between angels and loved ones for the purpose of this book. Angels are elevated beings who dedicate their existence to helping others with compassion and love. Loved ones who pass on to the other side differ from angels or spirit guides in one important respect. Loved ones work with angels to help family members or friends in the physical realm.

Unless they had a special passion or hobby, it is rare that a loved one would spend time helping strangers. This is usually the realm of angels. Angels help us with our spiritual development long term, while loved ones help us with our personal development short term. Nonetheless, angels and loved ones work closely together to achieve a vital balance between personal short-term goals and long-term spiritual development. Both play an essential role in our spirituality.

* * *

My mother's passing led me to discover another world, a world where hope and love are boundless. Imagine such a place and you are one step closer to receiving messages from your loved one. Just don't be surprised if your loved one says, 'What's the matter? I've been here the whole time.'

Step 2

Pay Attention to Coincidences:
Techniques to Cleanse Thoughts

Each of us has this moment. Some call it an epiphany. Others refer to it as an awakening. For me, I think it was closer to a reckoning. I spent many years turning away from my spirituality in an attempt to feel socially accepted. You see, it just wasn't 'cool' to talk about angels. Growing up, friends wanted to discuss boyfriends, music and movies. They were less than willing to discuss the deeper questions in life. It was only when I really began paying attention to the coincidences in my life that I found the happiness I desperately sought in my teens and realized my true path.

There are several ways you can learn to pay closer attention. You might want to try the following techniques to clear your mind and the space you inhabit. The more weighed down we are with painful memories, daily preoccupations or stressful thoughts, the less likely we are to notice the events occurring around us. Negative thinking is like a narrow alley. It constrains us to think in a certain way, inhibiting healing.

Techniques to Cleanse Thoughts
- Meditate daily.
- Listen to music.
- Keep your living space tidy.
- Avoid clutter, old clothes with bad memories, or photos of people that make you feel less than the best.
- Cleanse your body; cleanse your mind. A shower can help revive you.
- Take a holiday to a sacred space or natural park.
- Keep a journal. This will help you from revisiting

unhelpful thoughts. You can write a negative thought down and counteract it with a positive statement.

The Quest

Remember we are all special beings with a unique purpose. Transforming grief into guidance helps us to realize that purpose, freeing us from the preoccupations many of us experience after we lose a loved one.

Our journey is as much a story as it is a quest. The more you understand about your life day to day, chapter to chapter, the more you become aware of its direction and course. With this awareness you begin to connect the dots between time, place and person, and distinguish grief from guidance.

Throughout the 11 steps of this book I share my story and experiences to illustrate how I turned grief into a unique opportunity to receive guidance. My story shows how death can become a life-affirming experience by using many of the techniques, tools and exercises cited in each chapter.

A Childhood Memory

Spirituality was always an essential component of my story. My earliest recollection was of a conversation that took place with my mother. I was 5 years old. There was a perfect autumn sky, clear and crisp. My breath was visible on the window of the backseat, clouding the glass every time I exhaled.

Mom and I were driving home after dance class. I sat in my pink tutu and black leotard, looking up at the Milky Way. There were ten thousand stars dotting the night, casting their soft light over the darkened farmland. My mind instantly wondered at the magnitude of the sky, which held the moon and all the tiny sparkling stars. We were told in class that this was the kingdom of God, where heaven was and the angels lived.

My mind couldn't grasp the enormity of it. I found myself wondering aloud what heaven looked like.

'Heaven is big and white. People are very happy there,' Mom explained.

'Do people live in houses?' I asked.

She paused for a minute, before answering, 'People live in houses they build with their imagination.'

'What would our house look like?'

'Big and full of light,' she replied.

I imagined a transparent house with infinite rooms floating in the sky. 'A glass house!' I shouted with excitement.

'That's right, a glass house where we could see for miles and miles, and everyone we knew and loved would live with us.'

'Like Grandpa and my baby brother?'

There was silence, followed by a long sigh. 'Everyone will be there: your grandfathers, grandmother and baby brother.'

'Will you be there?' I asked under my breath, afraid of her response.

'I'll be there when it's my time.'

'But how will I know it's your time?

'I'll send you a sign.'

'What's a sign?' I asked. My face twisted with confusion.

'A sign is a message. I'll send you a rainbow to let you know when it's my time.'

* * *

Admittedly, I missed a few rainbows along the way. That's the problem when you don't pay attention. Skepticism gets the best of all of us, even me. Fortunately, I did not miss the breathtaking rainbow radiating from the window of the airplane, landing on my son's cheek as he slept. It was the first time I had visited the United States in 2 years.

As I boarded the plane, I thought how challenging those 2 years had been. My pregnancy was full of health scares, and the months after my son's birth were difficult. I struggled to adapt to the grueling waking-and-sleeping schedule of a newborn baby, all the while missing Mom terribly. It was hard not being able to call her to ask her if I had also suffered from colic. Dad wasn't much help in this department as he tended to have memory blanks concerning anything to do with me crying or needing to be changed.

'You really don't remember, Dad?' I asked in frustration as the clock struck one in the morning, another late-night emergency call. My question was greeted with silence, followed with Dad's defeated voice: 'Sorry, darling. I honestly don't remember.'

In these moments of desperation, I failed to understand that Mom never left my side. She was always near me, waiting for my questions, sending me signs to reassure me she was there. Not only was she near, but she also expressed the same strong opinions she did when she was living. She approved of our decision to spend Thanksgiving with my dad. Though it was a difficult journey, she wanted to let me know that she was proud of us for making the effort and remembering our American side of the family, *her* side of the family.

Mom never liked the rushed, commercial air that Christmas takes on during the holidays. The season of giving, or in most cases buying, never appealed to Mom, but Thanksgiving with its emphasis on family and gratitude always struck a chord. The fact that she passed away at Thanksgiving is significant in itself. Mom never wanted people to waste time grieving for her. She always said, 'You grieve not for me, but yourself', and I believe that she wanted us to celebrate life and count our blessings. I was reminded of this on our way to the United States. As the sun shone through a passenger's window, casting the most beautiful rainbow over my son's cot, I remembered the true spirit of Thanksgiving and just how many blessings I had to count.

My life had changed drastically since 2007, the year Mom passed away. There were so many things to celebrate. With my son, life came full circle. Even Dad found the strength to begin a new chapter of his life and start dating again. As I adjusted the blanket wrapped around my son, he turned his face away and I was struck by the beauty of the light. Fuchsia, yellow and violet illuminated his cheek as he slept peacefully. He stayed that way the whole journey, no small feat considering the flight was just over 9 hours and he was only 7 months old. That flight will be immortalized in my thoughts forever. It was our time, but more importantly, it was Mom's time. She sent me a sign, just as she had promised all those years ago under the beautiful night sky. I finally succeeded at turning grief into guidance. I was no longer burdened by feelings of guilt or resentment. I felt an incredible and lasting peace, which remains with me today. I call it a 'Circle of Light', the title of this book and also an allusion to the loving circle which protects and guides us at all times. When we become aware of this circle, we become aware of our true purpose. My personal story illustrates this deeply, which is why I've chosen to share it throughout the 11 steps to turn grief into guidance.

About Fate

I do believe we choose how, when, and where we die. Mom chose to die on Thanksgiving morning because she knew she could help me more from heaven than from the confines of a hospital bed. She made several predictions about her death that all came true in the end. I see this as further proof that there is a divine hand behind everything we see. Most of us are afraid to acknowledge it because it is simply too vast and frightening to conceive of, but when we look at all of the meaningful coincidences that occur in our life there is powerful reason to believe there is more to our lives than meets the eye.

The Skeptic's View

Some people may be sitting at this very moment reading this paragraph and thinking, *A rainbow—really? Does she honestly believe a mere projection of color is the work of a higher power?* The answer is 'yes.' I adamantly believe this is the work of a divine power. I am not here to debate the meaning of signs or whether or not they exist. The discussion I wish to present in this book is a discussion of the psyche, the emotional energy behind a person's life. The thoughts, feelings and memories we store up in a lifetime. Where does this energy go when we die? In the preface of this book, I discussed how the Cycle of Life and Death mirrors the Cycle of Grief. I am not proposing to know what life or death amounts to. I strongly believe life continues after death, but I would never claim to know what the ultimate goal of life is. Every religious text has its answer and that is the only answer most of us need. I am merely stating there is more to this life than we can possibly know in one human lifetime, a fact that has been acknowledged by countless thinkers and writers.

I want to turn the question on its head and ask all the skeptics, 'Do you think the cells in your body can conceive of you: the body, you: the person, you: the freethinking individual who they live within, fight for and fundamentally constitute?' No, they simply go about their routine, defending and building your body on autopilot. If they made allowances for all of the 'what ifs' in their existence, the body would shut down and self-destruct. Fortunately, much like our cells, I don't think we are granted access to the answers until we are prepared to receive this information.

Call it evolution; call it enlightenment, a quantum leap, a breakthrough. There are too many terms to count which might describe personal and collective growth, but until we experience these stages of growth we do not receive the answers. I know because I did not begin receiving messages from my mother until I was prepared to receive them, when I finally succeeded in turning grief into guidance.

The Importance of Preparation

You might ask yourself, 'But how does one become "prepared"?'

23

The answer is simple: pay attention. When I write 'prepared,' I use the word loosely to mean 'alert.' I don't particularly like the word 'alert.' It has an anxious ring to it. 'Mindfully awake' is a better description of the state of being I'm talking about. It's important not to go through the motions of life. Try to be aware of each moment as it unfolds and the significance it bears in your life.

I am not suggesting you should be constantly alert, but the idea is to be prepared enough to be sufficiently alert when something happens. Again, a journal can be very useful in helping you to prepare for the meaningful events in your life. If you keep a running entry of all of the coincidences in your life, you will begin to notice a pattern emerging, a theme or 'pathway.'

I found that the more you pay attention to the small coincidences in your life, the more likely you are to notice the connections between people, time, place and subject. This brings me to the very important notion of synchronicity. When we become aware of it, it can change how we witness events unfold, including the death of a loved one.

The psychologist and theorist Carl Jung first introduced the idea of synchronicity in his works about the human experience. He described it as groups of meaningful events that occur in a chain or pattern. Synchronicity suggests there are momentous coincidences in an ordered universe. In other words, the universe is not a meaningless void, as some philosophers would have us believe. It is a place of timed intersections or fate.

Have you ever noticed how a person enters your life just when you need him? When people say, 'It was the wrong timing,' or 'I was in the right place at the right time,' they are not far off the mark. The best example of synchronicity I can give occurred in a bookshop I used to visit without fail every month. It was located between Leicester Square and Covent Garden in central London. It stocked a wide range of secondhand books. Although the volumes were fraying at the edges and smelled faintly of mildew, there was something quaint about this bookshop. It never failed to draw me inside and downstairs where the bargain books were located. As the underground trains shook the walls of the shop, my eyes scanned the faded titles on the shelves. To my astonishment, I always found books on the subjects I had spoken with friends about only days earlier.

The most amazing book I found was an obscure work written by the widow of a scientist. It documented her communication with her husband in the afterlife, citing information known only to the deceased scientist as proof the contact was real and not fabricated. This book represented a turning point in my life. At the time, I was extremely conflicted about my faith and my promise to my mother to find someone who could give me a spiritualist reading. I grew disillusioned after being subjected to extortionate fees of $300 for an hour's worth of reading. No, I didn't pay this fee—because I simply didn't have the money and, looking back, even if I *had* the money I don't think I would have paid it out of principle. Anyone who has mediumistic talents has a duty to serve the public, not vice versa.

I knew, looking at the stark title of this book, *Love after Death*, that this was the sign and answer to the confusion and grief that had gripped me in the months after Mom's death. I dutifully bought the book and read it in just three sittings. The author was from London and spoke of receiving a reading at the Spiritualist Association of Great Britain (SAGB). My heart beat faster as it dawned on me that this association might still exist. I couldn't believe it. Just days earlier, I had spoken to my husband about the promise I had made Mom. I worried I wouldn't be able to keep it. Now, I had the chance. I was dumbstruck by the timing of this fortuitous coincidence.

On my return journey, the other passengers on the train looked at me with bland contempt as I stared out the window. The fog of grief lifted. I could see the connection. I felt Mom guiding me.

I hurried home to 'google' the SAGB. To my amazement, I found the association was very much active in London, giving readings for just £30 (ca. $50), a sum very much within my means. I read the history of the organization carefully. I was suspicious of anyone claiming to give readings. It was a credible association, a registered charity with a history dating back to the 1880s. It even had a church on site. Here was the sign I had sought for months. The universe had heard my prayer of lament and now the solution was right in front of me. I sat staring at the computer for a few minutes. My stomach twisted with indecision. No longer could I say it was impossible for me to find someone who could give me an affordable reading. My excuses were fast running out. It was time to honor the promise I had made to Mom. I called and made the first appointment available.

A Leap of Faith

'It was difficult for you to come today,' the man giving the reading observed. He had kind eyes. His voice seemed to linger in the air like a question mark. 'You have been very disappointed in the past with readings and it took a great deal of effort for you to make this appointment,' he added. I remained silent.

Do not respond to the person giving you a reading, especially if you are skeptical. If you must respond, try to limit your response to 'yes' or 'no.' Doing so ensures the reading is free from the influence of information or leading answers.

'I am glad you decided to give it a second chance and want to thank you for coming in today,' he continued. 'I see it is very important that I take the time to communicate everything I see, so that you leave this reading completely satisfied. First, I would like to say I have a lady here. It is your mother. Is this correct?' he asked.

I nodded to let him know this information was correct. The person he communicated with was indeed my mother.

'She is pointing to your hair. She wants to let you know that she likes it and that you look lovely. She is telling me this to let you know she is watching and is proud of you.'

This may not seem significant, but to me it was confirmation that Mom was around and very much a part of my life.

As I got ready to attend the appointment, I had looked in the mirror at my newly dyed brown hair and thought to myself with despair, *Mom would hate the way I look. She always loved me when I was blonde and now I have brown curly hair.* I don't know what possessed me to think this way, but it's the kind of thought one has in passing. Obviously, Mom heard and was now telling me that, on the contrary, she liked my new look. You might think communication with our loved ones through the help of angels is limited to revelations of the meaning of life and death. Often people imagine that angels appear in a flash of light and pronounce their name with a booming voice. Some angels do this. Generally, the more spiritually elevated ones move at faster speeds. These are the ones most commonly depicted in paintings and Hollywood films, but more often than not, our loved ones choose to speak about earthly topics: the daily ins and outs of our lives.

After all, it's the little things from which we derive the most comfort. The man who gave me the reading told me Mom had been trying to make contact for some time. Though she had already sent many signs, he reminded me that I also felt her presence near me at night.

'You might feel a wispy feeling on your cheek, as if there is a spider web or stray hair brushing your face. This is your mother's presence to reassure you she is near you,' he said.

In fact, the week before the reading I had batted the darkness because I felt the annoying presence of something on my cheek. I have a deep fear of spider webs. I was afraid a spider might be spinning a web near me. However, every time I wiped the imaginary webs away, they always returned with such warmth and insistence that it made me question the real cause of the strange sensation. I now knew it was my mother.

'Your mother is telling me she will send a sign with the help of the angels. Look for a white feather on your upcoming trip,' the man said at the end of the reading. 'Give her some time to arrange this. If you are near a bird aviary or a lot of pigeons and see a white feather, it is probably not a sign. It will be when you least expect it. Almost out of nowhere you will see a white feather.'

I tried to imagine how I might see the sign. Would a white feather be given to me by a stranger? Would my foot step on a white object that I would discover was a feather? How was it even possible for Mom to arrange this sign? Though I had seen other signs and suspected it was my mother, I had never had *this* kind of proof.

Here was a stranger who told me things about myself and my mother that he could never know. I had never met him nor did I disclose any facts or details about myself beforehand. My mother died in a different country under a different name; it would have been impossible to trace my history online or hers. This was the chance for Mom to really make contact.

As I walked back home, I found my eyes scanning the street for white feathers. There were none. My mind began to race with so many thoughts. Even though the man gave an accurate reading, doubt crept in. *Would Mom really send a white feather and how could I know it was her and not some coincidence?* I couldn't really conceive how Mom would arrange the sign, but somehow I held on to the hope and the belief she would make contact because this is what she had promised 2 years before in the hospital. I felt that she had made contact many times before, but here was the test we badly needed. It was time to see if Mom was really watching from above and if I could turn grief into guidance.

Step 3

Recognize and Interpret Signs:
Common Signs Loved Ones Use

My mother and I used to shout the lyrics of Don McLean's song, 'American Pie,' whenever we heard it playing on the radio. We loved music. The classic songs from the 1960s and 70s were our favorites. I lost count of the times we recited the lyrics from Bob Dylan's song, 'Like a Rolling Stone.'

Since her death, I haven't been able to listen to Dylan like I used to, but whenever I hear his music I am instantly transported back to my youth when Mom was alive.

They say music is the universal currency of love. When we remember a favorite song we used to sing with a loved one, we are reliving the past, which draws that person's soul closer to us. Have you ever turned on the radio and instantly heard your mother's or father's favorite song playing? If you have, then consider it a message. Don't believe me? Wait until you hear the same song a second or third time in the space of a week. Think it's a coincidence? As long as it's not a top-of-the-charts song, it probably isn't.

Try to calculate the odds of hearing the same song played as you enter a grocery store and on the radio as you turn the key in the ignition of your car. The odds are too great to calculate. There are a number of ways our loved ones try to communicate to us through the help of angels. Some of the signs are easy to recognize; others are harder.

Common Signs
- Favorite sayings heard on the radio, TV or in passing conversation
- Birds or shy animals that draw close without fear

- Feathers or coins left in meaningful places
- Insects associated with luck or beauty landing near you
- Rainbows or shooting stars
- A warm, calming presence
- Feeling your face or hand touched gently
- Sparks or sudden flashes of light
- Familiar odors like the scent of perfume or the pungent smell of cigars

Interpretation

Interpreting the meaning of these signs is never an easy task. Our loved ones often send us signs with the help of angels to reassure us or comfort us in times of doubt or need. They may send a sign to advise us or help us undertake a decision in a difficult moment. You should never ask for a sign for the purposes of entertainment or speculation. Signs are a divine language used for divine purposes. If you have any other intention, you will be disappointed. The angels are not here to entertain us, though many of them possess a sense of humor.

If you are having difficulty recognizing signs or feel frustrated because you believe you haven't been sent a sign, do not become disheartened. Our loved ones adapt to heaven at different paces. Some need more time.

Be patient and try different exercises. Keep a record of your experiences, so you can be objective about the occurrences in your life. Often our emotions get the best of us and we become frustrated because we are feeling insecure about life without our loved ones. Avoid frustration and negative emotions like anger; these feelings often prevent communication and delay our divine journey to turn grief into guidance and realize our true purpose.

The Importance of Timing

When Mom said, 'There are no coincidences,' I understand what she meant. The timing of some of the most important events of our lives is always momentous. Take for example the day I met my husband-to-be on a crowded train platform. The train was 20 minutes late. Normally, I would go home hours before. On Tuesday, my classes ended quite early. However, the new semester had just started and my friends had persuaded me to go out for a drink. I stayed for one drink, but was too annoyed to stay for a second because it began to drizzle—or 'spit' as the English say. On the way to the station, I discussed my love life with one of my friends. We walked under the drizzle, sharing an umbrella to shield us from the English weather. I remember saying that I wished I could find someone who really loved me for who I was, someone who was ready to settle down and build a life with me. My friend laughed and said I shouldn't take life so seriously; in time I would find someone. I was 19. I had a lifetime to figure out what I wanted. I agreed with her, but I couldn't help feeling she didn't quite understand the point I was trying to make. She said she would see me tomorrow. I waved goodbye and watched for a moment as she walked down the road.

I bought my ticket and descended the stairs. There were commuters standing all along the platform. I had never seen so many people. Much to my annoyance, I realized the train was 20 minutes late. The station was so crowded I could barely walk past the people scrunched together on the platform. I looked to my left and saw my future husband standing in a group of people. He was the tallest out of the group. He could not have looked more Italian, with his coat thrown over his shoulder. His eyes met mine and instantly I understood that we were meant to be together. I didn't question the thought. It was a fact which was obvious to me. I knew if I smiled, he would come over and ask for my number and we would spend the rest of our lives together. I also knew if I didn't smile, I would probably never see him again. I deliberated for a few seconds, before smiling. The rest is history.

My husband later told me that if I hadn't smiled at him he would never have approached me. He thought I was a bit of a snob, self-absorbed. Nothing could be further from the truth; I just hate crowds… and late trains. It's funny. My husband would have boarded an earlier train if it were not for a last-minute conference call from America which kept him in the office another hour.

The timing of our meeting is remarkable. What's even more amazing is that we recognized the importance of our meeting and acted on it. It is easy to dismiss coincidences as haphazard events, but when we pause to calculate the timing of encounters then we begin to understand that there is an invisible order behind our lives. Mom always told me, 'You must build your own life, Adele. You have very little family and you must create your own family. Marry well, so that you won't be alone after I die.' She used to say cryptic things like this all the time. At the time, I wrote them off as the babblings of an overprotective mother. I could never imagine that in less than 2 years after I met my husband and after only 5 months of marriage, Mom would pass away unexpectedly.

She always had a sense of urgency in her appeal for me to make my own family. I think she knew she would die younger than most. Passing on at 58, there were so many things she missed, like the birth of her first grandchild and seeing the four-bedroom house we bought in London.

Before Mom died, she told my husband, 'I know I can go in peace because my daughter has you. She's in good hands.' Mom's lifelong wish was to see me married. It sounds archaic, especially as fewer and fewer people choose to marry these days, but Mom valued marriage. To her, it was a serious affair: the lifelong spiritual, mental and physical union of two people.

When she told my husband that she believed I was 'in good hands', this was one of the biggest compliments he ever received from her. It equated to something like, 'I trust you with my daughter.' She gave my husband a hard time about being Italian.

It didn't matter that my father was French; Mom had standards and she wanted to let everyone know just how high they were. Despite Mom's initial doubts about the marriage, the three of us became close in the months after the wedding. We joked all the time and Mom referred to my husband as her 'son.'

With so much to celebrate, Mom's stay in the hospital came as a shock. We knew she was unwell, but we didn't believe she would die. How could we? Life had just begun for us. We wrote her prophecies off as the railings of someone who disliked hospitals. Though she had suffered a stroke and was half-paralyzed, her mind was fully intact and she seemed to be making progress with each passing day. From an outsider's perspective, she had every reason to be positive. Soon she would be sent to a rehabilitation center where she would learn to walk and sit on her own.

Passing Over

Looking back at it, I don't think any of us wanted to believe there could be truth in her cryptic predictions. 'I will die at the same age and month as your aunt. It's destiny,' she said, holding my hand. 'Do you remember when your aunt said I was next?' It's true; my aunt, my mother's sister, had spoken in her sleep towards the end of her life, predicting Mom would be next to go. She also mentioned the names of every loved one we had on the 'other side', and appeared to be in conversation with them.

She even held out her hand when speaking to my grand-mother (her deceased mother) at one point. She spoke like a child, 'I don't want to go.' My aunt fought her battle against cancer fiercely. She held on to life because she loved it so much. At the end of her life, she had become quite spiritual and inter-ested in spiritual phenomena. I recorded her predictions in a journal. When my aunt woke, she had no recollection of the conversations. 'But I didn't sleep at all!' she exclaimed. 'I couldn't have been asleep more than 10 minutes,' she protested. She had slept for 3 long hours.

I didn't want to believe my aunt's prediction was coming true. I shook my head and told my mother not to be silly. I calmly explained that she was afraid. We were all afraid.

'I have no fear. I just want to be released from this terrible pain I'm suffering,' she said, looking down at her hand. It was lifeless. Though we had hoped she might regain some feeling, she hadn't.

'Try to be positive, Mom,' I begged her. I couldn't understand why she was being so morbid.

'It doesn't matter. I've lived so much and seen so much. I traveled the world. I did things that no one did at my age.' When I didn't reply, she added, 'I've burned the candle of my life at both ends. This is why I'm here.' She sighed.

'I don't know why you're speaking this way. Mother, you're not going to die,' I insisted.

Mom ignored me. Staring at the November light pouring through the hospital window, she began quoting a favorite Dylan Thomas poem: 'Do not go gentle into that good night... Rage, rage against the dying of the light.' She paused, considering the words of the poem for a moment. 'My father raged. I'm done raging. I won't be like my father. I will go gentle into that good night.' She turned away from the window and looked at me for what seemed like an eternity. I wiped a tear off my cheek. 'You must promise me you'll find someone who can give you a reading upon my death. Don't let others dissuade you. I will have things to tell you and you alone. I'll be watching over you, protecting you. Promise me you will look for my signs,' she said, holding my gaze.

I couldn't look at her, so I stared out the window. 'I promise,' I replied, feeling numb. There was no getting through to her. She seemed adamant she was dying and yet I thought she must be suffering from depression. After all, it was natural to suffer from depression after experiencing a stroke and becoming partially paralyzed. I tried to understand her point of view. Part of me wondered why she didn't fight harder. A few days later Mom would be transferred to a rehabilitation center. I thought things would change. Mom would get better and eventually she would come home.

The day before Thanksgiving, my father and I went to the center to visit Mom. She voiced her desire to die once again. Except this time, it was with such insistence that both my father and I left the center feeling defeated. Before leaving, I washed Mom's hair and applied her favorite red lipstick and some concealer to hide her bruising. Her best friend was going to visit her that evening and I wanted to ensure she looked her best. Mom seemed to perk up after I helped her get ready. She told me I looked beautiful and that she was proud of me as always. I smiled. *Maybe she just needs to feel like herself,* I thought, trying to take comfort in the momentary change in her attitude.

That night, my father and I went to see the movie *Beowulf.* Mom would have loved the film because she loved anything remotely to do with literature. Part of me felt guilty that my father and I were enjoying the film, while Mom was stuck in the rehabilitation center. Yet what could we do? The scenes between Beowulf and his father struck me deeply. Beowulf's father was afraid and old, incapable of defeating the dragon that terrorized the village. It was up to Beowulf to save the village. He was alone, as every hero and person finds himself in the starkest trial, but somehow he defeated the dragon against all odds. It seemed there was a divine hand behind his victory. I left the movie theater feeling empty. My father and I both agreed it was a great film. We tried to make small talk... anything to distract us from Mom's suffering. We ate a cold dinner and went straight to bed. That night I dreamt of furious dragons and faraway lands. I slept deeply, but I can't say I slept well.

The following morning, I awoke to a sun-filled room. Though it was November, the sun was shining brightly. These were the kinds of days Mom loved. She called them 'diamond days.' I looked up and down the hall. The house was eerily silent. I called for Dad. There was no response, only deafening silence. It was ten o'clock, the morning of Thanksgiving Day. We were supposed to visit Mom together. I couldn't understand why he wasn't at home. I called his phone. When he picked up, he said, 'I'm glad you've called. I didn't want to wake you. Mom passed away at six this morning. They called me and I left right away. She had a fatal aneurysm that led to hemorrhaging of the brain. I'm so sorry, darling. There was nothing they could do. She died almost instantly.'

I don't remember what I said. I just remember hanging up the phone and looking at the Christmas tree twinkling back at me with naïve innocence, and the terrible strain of my heart breaking in two.

Losing a Loved One

Until you've lost someone, you won't know the raw animal emotions that come out of you. I began to wail, holler and shriek. The perfect silence of the house shattered. I hated the Christmas tree. I hated that Mom hadn't tried harder. I hated that it was Thanksgiving. Why was this happening to me? I would never see Mom again and yet I had seen her just a couple of hours beforehand. What if I hadn't gone to the film—would things have happened differently? So many conflicting thoughts raced through my head, but I couldn't walk. I couldn't escape the thoughts. I could only crawl on my hands and knees like some wounded creature.

My mother's best friend came to get me later in the morning. With her help, I managed to get ready. She cried while she hugged me and told me how sorry she was. 'Your mother seemed well when I visited her last night. She told me she would try to fight the stroke. She asked me where she could find a good nurse. She seemed as determined as ever.'

That wasn't the picture Mom had painted us. I didn't want to reveal how tortured Mom was in her final days. Instead, I simply replied, 'I'm so glad you were the last person to see her. I know she always gained so much comfort from your friendship.' I was growing up faster than I knew. A younger, less thoughtful me would have contradicted my mother's friend, but what was the point? Mom was in peace. Didn't we also deserve to be in peace? She had gone gently into the 'good night' just as she said she would. She passed away almost instantly from an aneurysm in her sleep.

Something strange happened while my mother's best friend and I were talking. She asked me when I thought my mom would try to make contact. Remembering my conversation in the hospital, I stammered, 'I don't know. Soon, I suppose, knowing Mom.'

My mother's best friend recounted her own experiences of her husband's death and the signs he had sent. Almost as soon as she began speaking, the room lights started to flicker. Even the Christmas tree stopped flashing for 3 seconds as the lights switched on and off. Was this the first sign? Was Mom trying to tell us she had safely reached the other side?

Her friend seemed to think so. 'Look, it's your mother! She wants to let us know she's here.'

We stared, looking up at the overhead light, before laughing. It was classic Mom, so insistent; unmistakable, really. Mom knew all along. She was light years ahead of the rest of us. Though she tried to tell us, none of us would listen. Now she had our attention. 'We got the message,' her friend smiled. Yes, we got the message.

The messages didn't dull the pain of grief, though. When you lose a person, you invariably lose a piece of yourself. As the reality of Mom's death sank in, it felt like small needles were pressing into my skin. I wanted to forget what was happening; yet, I was conflicted. I believed it was important to celebrate life, to remember Mom as she would want to be remembered. Mom was at peace. So why couldn't we be?

I could have spent Thanksgiving curled up in a ball feeling sorry for myself, but this was not what Mom wanted. I reminded myself that Thanksgiving was her favorite holiday. It was a time for family to gather around the dinner table and count their blessings. I rolled up my sleeves and cooked a Thanksgiving meal for the friends and family that gathered upon hearing the news. I wasn't completely myself. I sliced a small piece of my finger off as I chopped the potatoes. I bandaged it up with cotton pads and tape (my family never seems to have bandages) and forged on with cooking. I didn't allow myself to blubber in front of guests. Somehow, we managed to have a great Thanksgiving.

* * *

The journey to turn grief into guidance teaches us that life is meant to be celebrated, not mourned. Mom got to do everything she ever dreamed she would do. She traveled all over the world in the 1970s, a time when few women dared to travel, never mind travel unaccompanied in India and Yugoslavia. The world was not as connected as it is today. There was no Internet; long-distance calls were a luxury. Post was by far the most commonly used form of communication. Now, most of us think of the post as a novelty. If you receive a letter, it is something of a surprise. Life was very different in the 70s; if anything, it was more romantic. Mom was an adventurer, traveling on the Orient Express to visit faraway countries. She slept on the baggage rail to avoid unsavory male passengers touching her in her sleep. One Turkish man even showed her the long nail of his pinkie finger. He had grown it to sniff tobacco. 'Charming,' she replied to the smiling Turk before rolling her eyes and turning to face the window.

Did I mention Mom was beautiful? Yes, she really was, with blonde hair down to her waist. She had blue-green eyes that seemed to stare through you. I can't tell you how many countries she saw, far too many to count. She spent extensive time in Japan, Korea, Hong Kong, Italy, France, Belgium, Egypt and Algeria. She was excellent at riding horses. She won competitions all around the world. She rode Arabian military horses bareback in the middle of the desert with male trainers. Somehow, she persuaded them with her excellent horsemanship to take her with them. I think they thought she was secretly a man, though it helped being married to a diplomat and a doctor. Doctors were in very short supply in Algeria.

Mom was the classic daredevil. She was also incredibly generous. There was no one like her. She could make people laugh and cry in equal measures, usually at the same time. She had several sports cars. She burned through them. Their engines caught fire from being driven too fast. They were probably not well made in hindsight and didn't have the safety features cars do today. Mom had other interests. She was an expert in eighteenth-century antiques and ceramics. An avid bargain hunter, she amassed most of her collection for less than $20 apiece.

She was an amazing woman who set the bar very high for me. When loved ones like our parents pass away, we often have very big shoes to fill. Death challenges us to grow up and find ways to fill these shoes and the roles our parents and loved ones played in our lives. If we allow it, death can be a positive experience. However, we must first learn how to accept loss before we can truly heal.

Step 4

Accept Loss: *How Loss Can Positively Affect Our Lives*

There was nothing Mom didn't know. I learned a lot from her life, but most of all I learned never to take a passing moment for granted. Death and grief give you this perspective. Oddly enough, they invigorate you; as long as you don't allow yourself to become weighed down by guilt. Mom used to say that when bereaved people cry, they do not grieve for the people they lose as much as they grieve for themselves. Regret is a very human emotion. Our loved ones do not feel regret; they only feel love and compassion for those who hurt them when they were alive.

When you die, you are relieved of human emotions like fear, anger or hate. You feel at one with the divine. There is symmetry to your life. Your existence is at one with our collective divine purpose. Essentially, you understand the grander scheme of things. Our loved ones don't sweat the small stuff like we do. They suffer, mainly when we suffer; but unlike us, they don't endure suffering needlessly.

Some people enjoy suffering. It's not something most will readily admit to, but it's more often true than not. Look around at the friend who is always complaining that she hates her life, or the cousin who never can seem to get that promotion he thinks he deserves. Why do we continue to suffer, when the solution is at hand? It's a question I often ask myself. I think people suffer because they are afraid of being responsible for their lives, masters of their own destiny. Sounds counterintuitive, right? Surely, if the answer were staring them in the face, they would grab hold of it and change their life, right? Wrong! Grabbing hold of the solution is the same as taking responsibility for the decisions they made and the present course of their life. It is infinitely easier to blame someone else. 'I hate my life because no one loves me' or 'I haven't gotten a promotion because my boss doesn't recognize my hard work.' My communications with my mother taught me to annihilate these thoughts. I learned to replace negative thoughts with positive mantras.

Instead of thinking, *No one loves me*, think, *I love many people, and many people love me in return* or, *I will get the promotion I deserve because I deserve it, and others will soon recognize this fact.* We have all been stuck in a rut at some time or another. Some of us refuse to pick ourselves up and get out of this rut. Some of us permanently reside in this rut. If there is a medical issue behind your suffering, seek help immediately. This is perhaps the only veritable excuse. However, if you think you are suffering because you do not possess enough confidence or self-belief, know the answers are within, not without. Look in the mirror and ask yourself what you really want. Once you know, you can earnestly begin working towards this goal. Don't let the loss of a loved one slow you down on your divine journey; if anything, let it be a lesson to live your life more fully.

Other Techniques

• Ask for Help
This might come in the shape of a friend, sibling, partner or health professional. We all want to appear strong for family members and friends when we experience loss, but know that it is okay to be vulnerable. You can be positive and vulnerable at the same time. Often we need to expose our deepest emotions and admit that the pain we are suffering is real before we can find ways to confront the pain and change it into positive thinking. If you can remain positive, you are one step closer to turning grief into guidance.

• Be Good to Yourself
Above all, do not punish yourself mentally, physically or spiri-

tually. People often feel responsible for the passing of a loved one. They feel they are to blame or think the death could have been prevented in some manner. Banish this thinking. Your only responsibility is to cherish your memories of a loved one and honor his or her achievements in the best way possible.

• Get Creative

You too can write a book to record your memories. A scrapbook or short film also is a good way to process your emotions. If you want to feel really connected with the person you lost, consider pursuing a loved one's hobbies or passions. You don't have to become an expert in cars, for example, but you might want to consider starting a club or fund for people who enjoy cars in your dad's or brother's honor.

Making Space for Grief

Sometimes suffering is necessary. There is a time and place for grief. When the person you lose is your mother or father, you find yourself forced to grow up almost overnight. The barrier between you and the world shrinks. You feel every high and low more acutely as if your pain threshold has been reduced. When you lose a child, you wonder how you will continue to live your life. This is when faith becomes a crucial element of your journey. Though the passage is deep, wide and darkly lit, push through your fears and ask for guidance. The steep cliff is part of the journey. *This too shall pass.*

Make no doubt about it. Death is hard. It's hard because it reminds us of how little time we actually have on earth. It brings up so many unresolved issues within families and friends. A beloved's passing is often the catalyst for change in a person's life.

When my mother died, I planned the funeral, a eulogy, cleared out the house, and entertained friends and family. I had just turned 22 and suddenly I found myself playing the role of a much older woman, someone in her forties. Mom was not supposed to die in her late fifties. This was never the plan. Though I managed to contain myself in front of friends and family, I did cry to myself in the early hours of the morning. Really, I cried to Mom. I never doubted for a second that she was around. I just didn't know how much she was around.

Asking for Signs from the Angels

As I was getting dressed one morning, I recalled the conversation Mom and I had had in the hospital. 'Promise me you will look for signs after I die.' Her words rang over and over in my mind. I had made this promise, but what did it mean; how was I supposed to go about keeping it? I remembered reading that people often write letters to loved ones who have passed away. Maybe I could write Mom a letter, asking for a sign. But this was too vague. How would I know it was from her? It became clear to me; I must choose the sign, but a very specific sign might be too hard for my mother to send me. Asking for an orange bird to land on the car, for example, might be a little 'over the top.' I read that it is often difficult for newly deceased spirits to send signs, as they have not come to grips with the way heaven works in relation to earth. They often rely on angels to help them send messages. I decided to write a list of three signs my mom could choose from to send me. My simple handwritten list read:

- Blue dress
- Ladybug
- Purple iris

Each of these signs had a significant meaning to Mom and me, wrapped in a precious memory. I wanted purple irises for my wedding day. They were one of Mom's favorite flowers, but we decided they would wilt too easily in the Italian heat. In the end, we opted for traditional roses instead. Ladybugs have always been a favorite insect of my mother's. She liked the luck attached to them, and their bright, distinctive black-and-red coloring. Black and red were two of Mom's preferred colors. Though the blue dress was not significant to any one memory we had, Mom was always shopping for me, making sure I was well dressed. I reasoned that each of the signs could easily be used in conversation or be seen while walking down a road. Obviously, I wouldn't think the first blue dress or ladybug I stumbled on was a sign. It would have to be a sequence of signs, ordered in a meaningful way.

For instance, someone might mention ladybugs to me in a conversation about gardening. On the same day, I might see a ladybug charm on a little girl's bracelet. At the end of the day, I might settle down to a meal outdoors and find a ladybug near my plate as I discussed the previous sighting with my husband. I reasoned such a coincidence wouldn't really be a coincidence, but an instance of synchronicity and a message from above. Little did I know I was in for one of the biggest surprises of my life! I never dreamed Mom would hear my message, let alone answer my letter in such a big way, but then again she never did anything in a small, unassuming way. Whatever Mom did, she made sure it had an impact. She knew how to get an audience's attention and she did more than that in the days following her death. She made us believe again in the miracle of life.

How You Can Ask for Signs

You don't have to wait for a loved one to pass on to the other side to receive guidance. Each of us has angels protecting us and assisting us through difficult moments. They are eternally present to guide and direct us. Do not hesitate to ask for their assistance, as this is their divine purpose.

Connecting with a loved one can give you peace, especially if you had unresolved issues at the time of death. Angels help us continue conversations with our loved ones, reassuring us of their presence and their love; love we may not have always felt when they were alive. All of this is part of the healing process.

• **Decide what you want to ask.**
Be very clear and concise. A question like, 'What is my future?' is a little vague. 'Should I pursue becoming a therapist or an architect?' is a much clearer question. The clearer your question, the clearer your intention becomes. This is why it is important to clarify your thoughts and the way you feel about an issue before asking for guidance.

• **Trust your instinct.**
Remember it is wonderful to ask for guidance, but there are times when you need to trust your instinct. If you're asking loved ones for assistance, keep in mind that their advice might reflect the same thinking they exhibited when they were alive. So if Dad didn't like your boyfriend when he was alive, don't expect him to be converted on the subject. Sometimes we are alone for a reason. There is a vital lesson that needs to be learned.

• **You can wait for a sign or you can make a list.**
Maybe you want to enjoy the experience. If so, leave it to the angels to decide. The element of surprise allows amazing, unexpected experiences to unfold. Perhaps you are quite anxious by nature and don't want to leave any room for doubt. In that case, a list will give you a sense of order.

• **When you feel you have received your sign, make a mental note.**
Do you feel like things are falling together suddenly, almost miraculously? The angels are guiding you, and you have received their message. However, if you are feeling frustrated because the matter feels unresolved, don't hesitate to ask for a second sign.

Step 5

Document Your Journey: *Useful Tools*

Documenting your journey is a crucial step towards turning grief into guidance. Have you ever noticed it's only in hindsight that you understand why a situation happened? That is because thoughts are a complex arrangement of action and reaction. It is very hard to understand the relationship between action and reaction, cause and effect, in the heat of the moment. The mind needs time and more importantly space to understand the impact of an event.

When you lose a person, you need time and space to process the loss. Grief is complex. It's not unusual to experience anger, nostalgia, bliss and indifference in the space of a couple of weeks. These emotions occur with the loss not only of a loved one but also of a job or a cherished passion, or after a traumatic birth. When change occurs, we are often surprised how we or those closest to us react. Documenting these reactions will help give perspective amid the upheaval.

How you choose to document your journey is up to you. I began documenting my journey by keeping a journal. Please don't feel restricted to writing. There are a number of ways you can document your journey.

• Talk with Friends and Family
Often, we gain the most insight by sharing our journey with friends and family. A weekly conversation with a friend or family member in a coffee shop or on the phone may be all you need.

• Make Use of Social Media
Share your endeavors on a blog or through posts on an online forum. The Internet provides shyer people with plenty of oppor-

tunities to connect with likeminded individuals.

• Attend Workshops or Groups

Workshops and groups provide members with the time and space to discuss pertinent issues, often resulting in a 'breakthrough.' This is why I created Ask Angel Women's Workshop and the spin-off Ask Angel Partners. You would be surprised how much people can accomplish in groups. The outdated peer-group models of the 1960s and 70s have been replaced with dynamic and interactive workshops. If you can't find a workshop near you, start your own!

* * *

The Internet has brought people together in ways that previously would not have been possible because of barriers in community, ethnicity and age. There are fewer and fewer reasons to feel lonely in our ever-connected world. If you feel you aren't supported by your friends and family, reach out to a wider community of people which is only a click away. Just remember it is preferable to share information with legitimate groups that meet face to face in a safe environment rather than with an unregulated online community.

It's amazing how popular Twitter and other social networks have become. In 2007 Twitter was in its infancy and Facebook was predominantly used by students (its intended audience). I documented my journey in a very traditional way. I found myself writing letters or poems to my mother, coupled with sporadic journal entries. This was my form of therapy. One of the letters I wrote changed my life, transforming the way I thought, not only about the world, but also about my purpose.

Documenting My Journey

Though I had written Mom a letter asking for a sign, I didn't expect anything to happen.

'We will see,' my father pronounced in his French accent, something he has retained even after living in America for nearly 30 years. My father was open to the experiment. My husband nodded his head in agreement.

We went to bed, nearly forgetting about the letter until the following morning. My husband was taking a shower, getting ready for the memorial service, when a ladybug landed on his hand. He shouted my name: 'Adeeele!' I ran up the steps, assuming the water had run cold. 'Look!' he said as he held his wet hand out of the shower. I squinted and, to my amazement, saw a ladybug on his finger, the light reflecting off the drops of water on his hand. 'It's your mother,' his voice pronounced behind the curtain. I pulled it back and we both smiled.

Later, I was sitting on a chair in the bathroom, when a strange speck on the ceiling caught my eye. I instantly assumed it was a spider. Whenever there is a spider in the room, I need to get rid of it somehow. It's a compulsion I have had ever since I was a child.

My arm shook as I stood on the toilet in the bathroom. I held a piece of tissue paper in my hands with the intention of vanquishing the spot.

'What are you doing?' my husband demanded.

'I'm trying to kill this spider. I don't want it to fall on you. It could be poisonous.'

He sighed. 'Be careful. The last thing we need is for you to wind up in the hospital.'

As I leaned forward, I realized the brown dot was actually red with black spots. I was looking at a ladybug, not a spider. Its willowy outstretched legs looked like spiders' legs from a distance. 'It's another ladybug!' I exclaimed.

'What?'

'It's a ladybug, not a spider. I was about to kill it without looking.' I peered at the ladybug, trying to scoop it in my hand. I realized there was a second ladybug just next to the vent a few inches away. 'There's another one!' I shouted.

'Another one?' my husband repeated as he got out of the shower.

'Yes, another ladybug. That makes three.'

Three ladybugs in the bathroom was not a coincidence. I beamed. 'I can't believe it! I have to show Dad.'

I raced downstairs with my hand in a neat fist. The ladybug flew from my hand and landed on the wall behind my father. He began to cry.

I will never forget Dad's expression when I showed him the ladybug (or the first time he saw his grandson). In a way I was a messenger, delivering a very private communication between my mother and father. Mom sent the message for all of us, but most importantly she sent it to Dad. He was the one suffering the most.

Love Continues

I believe my parents were soul mates and love does not end because one person dies. It continues in so many ways. Just because you can't see the love doesn't mean it isn't there. It's in the smile of a grandchild or the simple joy of hearing your mother's favorite poem or seeing your father's favorite team play. You only have to look for the signs. It's amazing how distracted we can become by all the small things that fill our day, the worries and preoccupations. I almost squashed the sign my mother sent me, because I was so distracted by the preparations for her funeral.

I think people miss signs because they simply aren't paying attention. Our primitive ancestors were open to signs because life moved at a slower pace. Though life was shorter, preoccupations were fewer (at least the superficial kind that seem to permeate our society). People were closer to mortality and looked for reassurance in any way. Their faith was closer to their hearts.

A Divine Infestation

The sightings of the ladybugs did not end with the bathroom episode. They continued and grew in frequency. On our way down to bury my mother's ashes in the family mausoleum, we discussed the significance of the ladybugs. Little did we know the surprise that was in store for us in Quitman, Georgia.

When we arrived in Quitman, the town seemed deserted. We got lost several times *en route*, stopping at a gas station to ask for directions. The gas station was decorated with the various heads and feathers of animals the owner had shot. If memory serves me right, there was at least one rattlesnake. It must have been 4 feet long, preserved in its fierce state. It looked like the opening shot of a horror film, but it's not unusual in the backwoods of Georgia to find outposts like this. I remember as a child I often saw men walking around in overalls with nothing but what God gave them underneath, sweating in the 99-degree heat of South Georgia.

At Quitman we were treated to the sight of a chain gang, a group of prisoners. It was a sunny afternoon and they were grouped in a line out in front of the city courthouse. It was like some backward scene from the 1930s. There was a policeman with sunglasses overseeing them, shouting out orders in a severe drawl.

'What are they doing?' my husband asked in horror as he peered out the car window.

'They're prisoners,' my father explained.

'Why are they chained together?'

'So they won't escape.'

I didn't find the scene in Quitman very amusing. I watched the prisoners fade into the distance. Their figures on the hill were ominous. We pulled into a second gas station to ask for directions to the cemetery. No one seemed to know where the cemetery was, until a drunken man mysteriously appeared.

'I know where it is,' he slurred. 'Here, I'll get in and show you,' he said as he wobbled to the car. Much to my horror, he reached for the door to the backseat where I sat. My heart felt like it was about to jump out of my chest. The attendant in the gas station shouted at the man. He waved the attendant away with a flagrant hand and a few obscenities.

The town drunk, who was clearly not right in the head, was about to get into our car. He pulled the handle—and nothing. Mercifully, the door was locked.

'That's okay. We can find it on our own,' my father said after he recovered from his initial shock.

After a few wrong turns, we eventually found the cemetery, passing a long line of Southern gothic-style houses. They were hauntingly beautiful with tall oaks framing them on either side of the unkempt front yard. Spanish moss hung on every limb of the trees like unruly spider webs. The town was rotting, but I had never seen anything quite as picturesque. Even decay can be beautiful.

The cemetery was prettier than I remembered. It was full of Victorian statues of angels and slabs of marble. There were also a handful of war memorials dating back to the Civil War and more recently Iraq. A lake in the distance shimmered as a warm breeze swept past. I could hear the birds in the trees.

I took the key from my bag to open the mausoleum. It was an iron key, large and antique. I turned the great iron and bronze door. It turned with a groan like some ancient vault. I was a little scared. I didn't like the idea of the other bodies in the mausoleum. Who would?

As soon as I opened the door with a shaking hand, a flood of red overwhelmed me. There were two thousand ladybugs. I could barely breathe. The sight knocked the breath out of me.

If this wasn't a sign, I don't know what is.

The ladybugs could be considered an infestation, albeit a divine one, but how did they manage to crowd the mausoleum in less than 24 hours? This is a question I still ask myself today. I am sure a biologist could explain this event as a very common occurrence in the insect world.

The sighting of the ladybugs is, as Mom used to say, 'stranger than truth.' This was one of her personal sayings, replacing the popular phrase, 'stranger than fiction.' I am no expert, but I am certainly open to signs and the guidance they can bring in our lives, especially when we are recovering from loss. The faith that these signs instilled in my life has given it renewed direction. There seems to be a shape and purpose behind it which was previously missing.

My hope is that you too will find a renewed shape and purpose behind your life.

Step 6

Don't Lose Faith—Ask for Guidance:
Breakthrough Grief

There are times when we question our faith or beliefs. In these moments of doubt, do not retreat into seclusion. While it is tempting to go into hiding and stir over a dilemma, the best thing you can do is confront the dilemma 'head on.' Do not allow your inner self to become disheartened with grief or despair; ask for guidance. The angels and our loved ones are here to guide us and help us solve our deepest conflicts. It is all too easy to lose yourself in a dilemma, but remember no dilemma presents itself without a solution. There is always an answer to every question. It might not be the answer you want to hear, but with faith you can find the knowledge you seek.

Messages can even come through close friends. Sometimes, the higher voice speaks through our loved ones, friends and family. You may not hear the higher voice in the advice your mother or cousin gives, but listen carefully. You might be amazed to find the same message repeated in different ways.

Pay attention to repetition and coincidences; this is a form of contact from the divine. Learning to recognize and interpret signs can be a very challenging and at times frustrating task, especially if you are experiencing a great deal of change or the loss of a loved one. However, once you learn to recognize and interpret signs, the messages they yield will greatly enrich your life.

A Moment of Doubt

One late winter afternoon I finally allowed myself to succumb to a wave of grief. I call it a wave because it utterly engulfed me. I spent the whole afternoon in bed, crying; very unproductive. I should have been looking for jobs. I had quit my job during Mom's hospital stay. In retrospect, I am glad I did. The strain of the funeral really took its toll on me physically and emotionally. I was exhausted in the months following Mom's death. I wasn't depressed, so to speak, but the event was so enormous it left lots of questions circling relentlessly around my head. I was here to stay in Britain, but what kind of life could I build? I never imagined I would stay, and now my future was indeterminately placed in Britain.

What else to do but cry, cry from the enormity of it, from my intense frustration? I felt quite miserable and sorry for myself. Two things which I swore I would never be. If anything, Mom's death should have taught me to buckle down and be prepared to fight for the things that mattered. Easier said than done.

That's when I heard the softest knock next to my bed. The blinds were up. *Did I really hear a knock?* I wondered in-between my sobs. I looked outside; the garden was empty. Only the blossoms of the cherry tree floated in the air. The sky was grey and the trees were leafless. It was late February and the light was pale. In a couple of weeks it would be spring, but looking around the garden you would never know. The room was silent. Nothing had produced the knock.

I heard a second knock and turned away from the wall. Suddenly, I heard chirping. There was a robin perched outside my bedroom window. It was the most timid-looking creature with a rust-coloured chest. I could almost see the bird's tiny heart beating through the feathers of its chest. Strangely, it did not look afraid. It looked full of life. It was inches away from me. It is often said that robins are relatively unafraid of human beings, but I never saw a robin that didn't fly away from me when I was in the garden. If the window had been open, I could have touched it. The robin sat looking at me for what felt like an eternity, with the kindest look in its beady eyes. I had never seen a bird so close, let alone a bird that looked at me so warmly, almost as if it knew me.

I didn't have time to smile. It chirped again and flew away.

I have never before and never since seen a bird so close. It was truly miraculous and I like to think my Mom sent me the little robin. She thought birds were very spiritual creatures, wise and hearty little souls. She loved robins. They always brought her a lot of joy, and in that moment I also felt joy, remembering my childhood and how we liked to watch the birds in our garden.

Once, a pair of robins built their nest next to our house in a crape myrtle tree. I think they misjudged the location, thinking it more private than it actually was. As we peered out of my dad's office, the birds caught our eye and realized the location of their nest was no longer a secret. The pair of robins abandoned their nest and tragically we found three bright blue eggs near our door. They had fallen from the nest and been smashed.

I saved the eggshells for a couple of weeks. I was incredibly sentimental as a child. Though it hurt me to look at them, it was also a poignant metaphor for the fleetingness of life. Three robins could have been born; instead, all that remained was the broken shells. I think I understood the significance of the moment long before I actually understood how and why people die. Each of us has these moments in our life when we understand the incomprehensible. The day I saw the robin outside my window, it was more than just a coincidence or even a sign. It was a reminder that life can come full circle and when one entity passes away, there is always new life.

Receiving Guidance

Some of us receive guidance more easily than others. I cannot say I have always received help as well as I should. I am so resistant to the idea of others helping me. If you are anything like me, recognizing guidance, whether it is spiritual or physical, is not an easy task.

The best way to receive guidance is to be in tune with your emotions. The guidance will come easily if you accept that you are feeling lost or helpless. Remember in the first chapter when I said angels need to be invited into your life before they can help you? The same is true of emotions. Emotions must be accepted before healing can occur. This is a vital part of the grieving process. If we accept and live alongside our feelings, we not only make space for grief in our lives; we also make space for spiritual growth. The day I spotted the robin outside my window was what therapists call a 'breakthrough.'

Ways to Achieve 'Breakthrough'

Breakthroughs, whether they are emotional, physical or spiritual, all rely on one common element: they involve breaking a habit. I was in the habit of not relying on others. The day I accepted my emotions and grieved for my mother was the day I experienced a 'breakthrough.' Not only did I accept my emotions, but I also received guidance; something I previously found difficult.

So how did I do it? I did something I rarely do. I sat in bed and cried. I don't recommend this as a solution for everyone, but I have spent my life finding ways to distract myself from my feelings. The more productive I am, the better I feel. I have less time to think about how I really feel. It is an elaborate avoidance technique. I avoid my feelings through action. In my case inaction was the solution. I allowed myself to be paralyzed by my emotions.

In hindsight, I wish I had a healthier balance between my feelings and my ambition, but this balance has improved over time. If you are someone who has the opposite problem and suffers from inaction, try a busy day of frenzied activity, involving all those minute tasks you have avoided. By breaking certain habits or behavior, you will be better positioned physically, mentally, emotionally and spiritually to understand your dilemma and grow in the process. Here are a few suggestions on how to break a habit.

• **Become an Active Participant in Your Life**

Begin and end your day differently. For example, if you watch TV every night before bed, try replacing the time you normally watch your favorite program with a journal entry. Instead of passively viewing a program, you are actively recording and processing your thoughts and feelings. The same is true of a daily commute. Instead of listening to the radio, purchase an audiobook on a subject that has always interested you.

• **Take Time Out**

When we take time out from our busy schedules to focus on our needs, we make space not only for grief, but also for our feelings. A simple bath or walk in the park may allow enough time for you to tune in to your feelings. If you are really stuck in a rut, plan a short trip away to a relaxing retreat. Consider taking the trip alone to really benefit from time out of your schedule.

Note: However, if you spend a lot of time on your own, a trip with a friend or family member may be just what the doctor ordered.

• **Join a Group, Workshop or Course**

Joining a local group, workshop or course is an excellent way to break out of a routine, meet new people and exchange ideas. While it may not help make space for grief directly, it will change your perspective and increase your confidence levels. Perspective and confidence help us move on with our lives and are important factors in the healing process.

Note: You might consider joining a group, workshop or course after you process your feelings. On the other hand if you join a group of likeminded individuals, you may find this support vital for sharing and understanding your feelings.

A Turn of Luck

The sighting of the robin propelled me to get out of bed and to find solutions. I began applying for jobs relentlessly. I felt Mom behind me, helping me along the way. Even when I didn't want to apply for a job, I felt someone pushing me, urging me to apply for it on the off chance I might get an interview. It was with this thinking that I applied for a 'merchandiser's assistant' role and finally got my first job working for an iconic British womenswear brand. I was reluctant to apply for the role as I was not keen on math. However, something persuaded me and I hit the 'send' button.

I attended a lot of interviews. There were moments when I thought I might never get a job, but I got lucky with a manager who would later become my friend. She gave me a little extra time on the math test.

Success! I finally had my first job working for a very good company. I was propelled into the luxurious world of fashion. I wasn't designing, of course. I was in the back office analyzing sales figures and forward-planning the collection for the next year. It wasn't as glamorous as some imagined, but it was a good start. My husband and I toasted to my success and I finally felt I was on my way.

In-between jobs, my husband and I moved to a bigger house. As soon as I saw the house, I knew it was the home we always imagined we would find. I was even surprised to see a pond full of carp, my mother's favorite fish. She had always loved oriental art and longed to own a bowl of koi fish. She never fulfilled this dream, so I was delighted to see a pond full of large carp, some of which were so big they looked like salmon. Their gold and red skin shimmered in the afternoon light.

It was another meaningful coincidence. This was exactly the kind of house my mom would have loved. It looked strangely like my childhood house, which was a copy of an English house from the 1920s. We were about to buy the real thing. A heron, a great swooping bird with long grey feathers, flew over the pond.

When I returned to our flat I saw the same great bird flying over the car. It landed in a nearby tree. *How strange*, I thought. It was as if it had followed me from the house. I took it as a good omen. The sale went through without a hitch and we moved in May 2010. We were finally ready to start planning our own family. The house was spacious. We liked the location and also the neighbors. All the ingredients seemed to be there, yet I found it incredibly difficult to fall pregnant. I began to worry. It had been 2 years since we first decided we wanted a baby.

Listening to the Message

Different friends gave different advice. No one seemed to have a clue why I couldn't fall pregnant, except my best friend.

'Your lifestyle is all wrong. You'll never have a baby living the lives of two people. You're stressed and your body won't support a child,' she told me. I looked at her intensely for a moment. 'What?' she demanded in a brash tone.

'You sounded exactly like my mother when you said that.'

'Is that so? Well, sometimes I think I feel her presence,' she confided. 'It's my role to tell you the things she would have told you if she were alive.'

My friend was right. After numerous tests it turned out there was nothing really wrong with me. It appeared stress was truly the culprit. Luckily, my contract at work ran out in a couple of weeks. I would be free of the stifling office that I had grown to dread every morning.

I finished my last day at work and packed the following night for our summer holiday in Cornwall. Little did I know that everything was about to change. Though I had passed the initial stages of grief, I had yet to truly receive guidance in a life-changing way. The test was about to come, but I was not as prepared as I could be. Although I had learned to love, I had not learned to pay attention to the signs that were all around me. This would have stark consequences for my future.

Step 7

Be Skeptical, But Don't Let Fear Get the Best of You: *Counteract Doubt*

I have struggled with skepticism all my life. In the first chapter I spoke about my struggle to learn to love. I likened love to a kind of innate faith. Even though I've successfully integrated spirituality into my life and healed from the grief of losing my mother, I still have moments when I question every bit of information presented to me. I also have a tendency to doubt others' feelings for me. I need to find a reason or purpose why I am in someone's life. Everyone has these thoughts from time to time. It's okay to have doubts. You may wonder if there really is a higher power or if love in its highest altruistic form truly exists.

But when doubt habitually sabotages your chance for happiness, this is a sign you need to reassess your thinking. While skepticism can be a useful tool, it should be paired with the right values.

Counteracting Doubt

• **Let others take the lead.**

Skeptics often find it hard to let others take the lead. Have you ever tried falling backwards into someone's arms blindfolded? This is a common exercise used in team-building workshops. A skeptic would have a hard time completing the exercise. Skeptics simply can't let go or trust others to take the lead. When we let other people make decisions in our relationships, this builds trust. Trust is like faith. If you struggle to let others make decisions, start with small tasks to build a better rapport. Once you've learned to let others take the lead, try bigger responsibilities. Taking a small leap of faith leads to bigger breakthroughs.

• **Quiet your mind.**

Skepticism is like a little voice that never stops chattering. Every situation a skeptic encounters has invisible subtitles, voicing doubt. Can you imagine how distracting this must be? If you are too busy questioning others' actions, you will never live. Skepticism undermines enjoyment of the moment and more importantly healing. Learn to quieten that pesky voice that is intent on analyzing people and situations. If you can quieten your thoughts, you are one step closer to appreciating the moment and letting go.

• **Learn to distinguish the higher voice from the ego.**

We are all programmed to think in a certain way. This starts at a young age, when our parents teach us to distinguish right from wrong. Learning to separate the higher voice from the ego isn't about distinguishing right from wrong. It is about determining what thoughts come from a loving place and what thoughts come from a fearful place. The ego is jealous and controlling. The ego does not protect; it undermines trust. This is why it is important to understand whether a person's skepticism originates from the ego or the higher voice. The higher voice is the voice of justice and reason. It wants to serve as much as it wants to protect. While the ego can drive us towards a goal, it is the higher voice which helps us heal and grow.

• **Confront doubt.**

Doubt serves a purpose in each of our lives. It is the way we balance our spirituality with the reality of daily life. However, if you constantly rely on doubt to make decisions, it quickly becomes a deficiency. Your perspective on issues becomes distorted by skepticism. The best way to confront doubt is to question your thinking. If you constantly find yourself wondering why people want to be your friend, ask yourself why you feel the need to question people's reasons for being your friend. Skepticism is a seed. It needs fertile ground to thrive. Turn the earth of your thoughts over and you will find it difficult for the seed of doubt to take root.

• **Try new things.**
Much like grief, skeptical thinking sometimes gets the best of us. Break the cycle by going to a class or workshop you would never previously have thought of attending. Try something new.

A Skeptic's Story

The man who gave me the reading at the SAGB told me my mother would send a sign. I hadn't forgotten the reading or the fact that Mom was supposed to send a sign. Even after the sightings of the ladybugs, I remained skeptical. I went to the SAGB looking for answers, but I was dissatisfied with the reading. I felt I wasn't any closer to getting the answers I craved.

A couple of weeks passed after the reading, giving me time to digest the information. I hadn't seen a white feather. I was still waiting for the sign, the test to see if Mom was present in my life. My husband and I decided to visit his parents in Sicily. It was January 2010 and bitterly cold. The Mediterranean winds turned icy and the piazzas were deserted. We walked the tiered coast, the sea churning fearfully below us. My hair swept around my face as I dared to look over the sea wall at the battered fishing boats below.

Now as I walked over the ancient cobblestones of a Sicilian village, I remembered the man who had given me the reading, and his words. I felt Mom's presence. She would have loved Sicily, the old churches littered with Caravaggio paintings and relics of the past. Sicily is a place that whispers a thousand secrets, but I love it in winter when it is deserted, when I can think in peace, and the only noise you can hear for miles is the rush of the sea and the howl of the wind.

On one of the last days of our trip, we walked through the

streets of the village, Noto. I sat on a bench to tie my shoes. An elderly nun joined me and we sat in silence, admiring the sun-filled streets. It was a beautiful day. There were more tourists out than on the other days. It didn't even feel like it was winter. As I tied my shoes, I noticed a white feather next to my heel. I was quick to dismiss this feather, remembering the advice the man gave in the reading: the feather would be placed in a significant way almost as if it appeared from nowhere. This feather had hardly appeared out of nowhere. The skeptic in me argued that it wasn't unusual to find a feather near a bench, especially in Italy.

'What a pity your mom couldn't see this! Isn't Sicily amazing?' my husband asked, pointing to the church. As he was pointing, the most beautiful feather fell peacefully from the sky. We were in the middle of the street far away from ledges or roofs. I didn't see a bird for a mile. I wasn't quite sure how it appeared. I looked up at the white feather drifting down from the clear blue Sicilian sky. It was a beautiful moment. No painter could capture it.

We saw another white feather a year later near Assisi. We walked behind a church to get a closer look at the beautiful garden behind the abbey. It was lined with a row of columns. It had several palm trees and the reddest geraniums I have ever seen. Set against the blue mountains, it was truly an amazing sight.

We hugged in the street and said how much my mom would have loved this village, particularly this secret garden we had stumbled upon behind the church. Without fail we looked up and a white feather floated down. Again, it fell from the sky away from any ledges, and the street was completely silent. No birds or people were anywhere to be seen. There was little to explain the unexpected appearance of the feather, not even a breeze.

Each appearance always happened just as my husband and I

spoke about my mother, expressing our wish that she could be there to enjoy the scene with us. It was an act of synchronicity which was nothing short of a miracle. It was the sign we had long awaited, the test the man who gave the reading devised to show my mother was really with us. Few could claim it was a random coincidence; if anything it was a meaningful coincidence that pointed to something even more compelling: the continued presence of my mother in our lives.

Finding Your Moment

You too can have a unique, life-changing experience with the divine. Skepticism can prevent us from paying attention to life's little coincidences. I am not sure I would have noticed the feathers in London. Going away on holiday allowed me to open myself to new experiences. If you are having difficulty receiving signs or messages, take a break. You don't have to go to Italy to have a spiritual experience. Consider visiting nearby towns with scenic parks or lakes. A change of scenery does wonders for the mind. When we are relaxed, we can reconnect with our spirituality.

However, I would like to issue a gentle warning to readers. Please don't overthink every coincidence in your life. The meaning should be obvious. In the opening chapters of the book, I mentioned the importance of being mindfully awake throughout the day in order to recognize and interpret signs from the spiritual world. I likened it to a state of being alert, but I don't want to encourage anxious over-analysis of every moment. It should be as natural as watching and interpreting a film. You wouldn't normally watch a film from a critic's point of view, obsessing on every narration, angle and scene. Please don't obsess over the events of your life in an attempt to squeeze meaning from a strange encounter. The meaning should unfold naturally. The significance should be second nature, like a message in a dream. You might forget the message, but it will reappear unexpectedly as easily as you forgot it. When we force meaning, it rarely comes.

The Test

Our travels in 2010 and 2011 pointed to a much larger theme playing out in our lives. We weren't the only ones devising tests to see if I was pregnant. It seemed we were also being tested by a higher power. Our lives were about to change forever.

After our holiday in Cornwall, I attended an important job interview. I was certain I had gotten the job. After the meeting, I walked around Hyde Park for a little bit. I felt very strange. My head spun, churning with thoughts.

I had wowed the interviewers with my knowledge of distribution, costs control and entrepreneurism; yet I didn't feel triumphant. I felt vacant like I couldn't quite concentrate. I was sure I was sleepwalking through London. What was going on? I didn't know what to do. I sat for a while on a park bench, watching traffic pass by and black cabs drop off their passengers. A jogger sat down next to me. He smiled and tied his shoe. I looked down and realized there was a gigantic white feather near my foot. It reminded me of the reading I had had nearly a year earlier at the SAGB, which was just off Hyde Park Corner (the organization has since moved to Victoria). Was this another sign? I was only a few blocks away.

Maybe Mom had something she wanted to say to me. She could help me figure out if the job with the American company was the right opportunity for me. On a whim, I made an appointment with the SAGB. The next appointment was in an hour's time. I decided to walk down to Knightsbridge and browse the shops in the area. On the way I passed a pharmacy and bought a pregnancy test. Something urged me to take the test before the reading. I walked into the Harvey Nichols department store in Knightsbridge and went up to the women's floor, where I knew there was a public toilet.

To my surprise the test yielded a very distinct cross—a positive result. 'What?!' I shouted to myself in the toilet. 'Impossible,' I declared. I could hear a woman coughing next to me. I was genuinely surprised and a little angry at the test I held in my hand. I felt it was playing games with me. It was always negative and now suddenly the stakes had changed. When and where did I get pregnant and how was the test already positive? It takes at least 3 weeks for a test to show a positive result.

Perfect timing, I thought to myself. *I ace an interview with a dynamic American company and the same day I find out I'm pregnant.* What could this mean? Maybe the white feather was a sign, if only I had realized sooner. What was the message the angels were trying to communicate to me in the toilets of Harvey Nichols? After a good 20 minutes, much wall-staring, intense mental deliberation and a few angry texts to my husband who wasn't picking up his phone, I decided to leave the store. *What next?* I thought. I was at another crossroads. But it didn't feel like a crossroads; it felt more like a roundabout.

I had already made the appointment with the SAGB for a reading. I couldn't cancel. There wasn't enough time. So I sat down again on the same park bench and took a few minutes to think over my life. My husband and I had tried for a baby for 2 years. In those 2 years I believed I might never fall pregnant. People, friends and relatives told me not to worry, that I would fall pregnant instantly. They were wrong, despite me charting my entire ovulation cycle for 2 years. No amount of planning quickened the process.

Now my dream had finally come true at the expense of another. I was never going to be a high-flying executive. I was good at the jobs I held, but they never gave me that extra spark. Yet, even as I sat on a bench in Hyde Park Corner, I couldn't help feeling something was at stake. I felt I had to make a choice and in making that choice I closed a door to another life, an alternative reality.

Learning to let go is hard. I gripped on to my former life with white knuckles. I couldn't let go of the life I had made after Mom's death. It was the life which had seen me through the grief and confusion that gripped me in the months after her death. At the same time, it was a life I had built to please others, to assimilate into my generation's idea of success. Like many, I went through the motions of my life on autopilot, not really pausing to consider my course. Now, this was the test. This was the shake-up I badly needed. It was clear I couldn't go on drifting, pretending I had a career.

My hands were growing cold from the autumn chill. I left the park bench and made my way to the reading. Unfortunately, it wasn't the best reading I ever received. Everyone has off days, and the man I saw wasn't particularly sympathetic to the chaotic energy I brought into the room. I can be intensely negative when I think I have to make a choice. The man who gave the reading picked up on this and asked me why I was making the decision more difficult than it had to be. He accurately saw that I was pregnant and that Mom had sent the white feather only moments earlier. However, he couldn't quite understand why I was making such a fuss about the news. It was something I had wanted for 2 years. It was news worth celebrating. *Shouldn't I be happy?*

I was happy, but for the first time I felt acutely responsible for the outcome of my life. I no longer saw myself as a haphazard consequence of events. Instead, there was this little notion of free will. I had always wanted to help people. Was I still going to be able to do this with a baby? The man who gave the reading assured me I would in time, but that I needed to take a deep breath and take each moment life gave me in stride. I could tell he was growing frustrated with me. He felt he couldn't get through to me. He wasn't the only one.

Weeks earlier, I had dreamed of my mother during our summer holiday in Cornwall. I received a message in the dream:

that I had conceived a child. Yet I chose to ignore the message. The skeptic in me argued that the dream wasn't real. I was certain that in my desperation to have a child, I had imagined my mother giving me a message. Later, believing I could never fall pregnant, I had several intrusive medical tests. These had actually risked my pregnancy; I should have lost the baby, but this thought hadn't sunk in yet. I was too worried about what the pregnancy meant.

The man giving me the reading turned to me and asked me rather sharply, 'When are you going to write your book?'

It was the kind of question Mom would ask, but I disregarded the question. I knew what she meant by this; I just didn't think it was *that* important. I felt both she and the man giving the reading were missing the point. So I nodded and answered, 'Soon.' This was a favorite word of mine. It was the magic word, which left hope I would complete the project, but didn't commit me to finishing. I didn't understand that in this reply, I was the one who missed the point.

Step 8

The Three 'A's: Attend, Attune and Attain: *Achieve Spiritual Goals*

If you take one thing away from this book, it should be 'The Three "A"s.' Over time, I've learned the importance of attending, attuning and attaining spirituality. This process is never complete. We are in flux: as we change, so do our needs. Each of us has a goal or life purpose. Realizing this goal happens in stages. You cannot attain a goal without attuning, and you cannot attune without first attending to your spiritual needs. Each of these steps represents a point on a circle. The circle never begins or ends, but turns and shifts to accommodate growth. It expands outwards as our consciousness evolves, reaching new heights of spiritual awareness; think of it as your very own spiraling staircase.

Attend

Attending to your spiritual needs can be challenging when you are grieving or reconnecting with your spirituality. It is important you make space for your spirituality in the form of development circles, journal entries, workshops, or conversations with close family and friends. This doesn't just mean documenting your journey; it means integrating your spirituality into daily life. Over the years, I've failed to attend to my spirituality for a number of reasons. It was only after I became pregnant that I was forced to integrate my spirituality into everyday living. In the previous chapter I spoke about how skepticism can impede our journey to become more spiritual. While it is good to question the events we experience, doubts can distract us from attending to our spiritual needs. Make sure you strike a healthy balance between your spiritual needs and your day-to-day needs. This will help you attune.

Attune

Do not neglect to attune to the higher voice. I spoke in the earlier chapter about the difference between the ego and the higher voice. The higher voice represents love, insight and guidance. The higher voice is located within your psyche. It is the voice that speaks autonomously and freely without your input. When this voice speaks, it often silences the ego and our daily preoccupations. It is pure and wise. It does not answer to fear, suspicion or aggression. Think of it as an omnipresent force, which is located within the psyche and without. When we attune to the higher voice, we are taking part in a much larger conversation which unites each of us.

There are specific exercises to help you attune. I have outlined some of these exercises in the section entitled 'Techniques to Cleanse Thoughts' in Step 2. Attuning is as much about cleansing thoughts as it is about finding paths to connect with the divine and receive guidance. There are a number of ways you can connect with the divine through signs, dreams and the messages they contain. It is important to note that a goal is different from a sign. Signs give confirmation. They assist in determining your life purpose, but they shouldn't be considered goals in themselves. If life is a highway, signs are simple road-posts. They might point us in the right direction, but they are not the destination of our spiritual journey nor are they necessarily an indication that we have truly transformed grief into guidance.

It is down to us to take control of our lives and exert free will in the vital decision-making process we encounter on a daily basis. Part of transforming grief into guidance depends on how much free will we exert. If you are passive about your life and the decisions you take, you will be passive not only about grief, but also about healing and spiritual growth.

Remember: *If you have a specific goal you would like to achieve,* *call upon the angels for help. There are a number of ways you can attune. As mentioned before, praying, meditating or writing letters outlining your goals are all excellent ways to tune in to guidance. Your goal may be to heal or make a new life. These are both positive goals. However, make sure to include timelines and specific dates by which you would like to realize your goals. It is important to be as specific as possible, so the angels can truly assist you in achieving your goals.*

Attuning with the Help of Dreams

They say angels visit us when we need them most. Dreams often yield solutions to our deepest dilemmas. The night I dreamed of my mother I felt considerable unrest. I was due to undergo a few exams to understand why it was so difficult for me to become pregnant. I fell asleep easily, but I think a lot of questions were racing around my head. This is why Mom chose to appear in my dream.

Over time, I learned to tell the difference between an ordinary dream and a dream that contains a crucial message. Dreams with messages from loved ones feel like real conversations. There may be some nostalgia connected to the dream, but it should be little in comparison to the feeling that the dream was so vivid that you were sure the conversation really took place. You may not remember the dream right away.

Often the memory of a dream comes back to you in phases throughout the day. You might be drinking a cup of coffee and think, *Wait a minute — didn't I speak to Grandpa last night?* Your conscience will immediately contradict this statement, reminding you that Grandpa passed away 3 years ago. You couldn't possibly have spoken to him and yet your dream was so real that for a moment you believed you saw him. This is the way I felt when I woke up.

I remembered my mother spoke to me. Her face was pale and her eyes were stark blue. It's not the way she looked when she was alive. In fact she was little more than an impression of herself. Really, she was a body of light. Her eyes locked with mine and I could hear her thoughts. Our minds were engaged in a mental conversation. Her eyes were startlingly bright. They shone like two lighthouses from a distant land. Though the dream was surreal, the message was very real. Mom said I would be pregnant in a week's time.

Angels and loved ones have different reasons for visiting us. Sometimes it is to reassure us they are okay. You might dream of your loved one smiling. They might even say, 'I'm okay. Don't worry about me.' In my case, I needed help. I didn't need to be reassured Mom was okay. I knew this all along through her signs and the other messages she sent. I was looking for clarity, which Mom gave me in the dream. My purpose was clear, but did I listen? That is another story.

When Skepticism Prevents Attuning

After Cornwall, for weeks I harbored the hope that I might be pregnant. Every test I took came back negative. I became even more frantic and obsessed with finding an answer to my infertility. I consulted a specialist. The fertility expert said he could see little wrong with me from the initial ultrasound, but he would refer me for additional testing. Now I sat outside the examination room, waiting for my name to be called.

The nurse looked apprehensively at me. 'Are you sure there is no possibility you could be pregnant?' she asked for the third time.

I was pretty sure the odds of me being pregnant were slim to none. Yet I hesitated. Why did I hesitate? The nurse sensed the doubt creeping over me. I looked at the calendar on my phone.

'I'll give you a minute,' she said, 'but if there is even a 1% chance you could be pregnant, you shouldn't undergo this procedure as you will most likely lose your baby and you don't want to risk *that*. You've already experienced difficulties conceiving. It would be a real disappointment.' She frowned.

I began to frown too. I had never had a nurse speak to me so directly. It threw me for a moment. She seemed to be imploring me to reconsider. I should have listened, but I was too consumed with skepticism. I went over the facts in my head a second time. I couldn't be pregnant. I had taken tests after Cornwall. They were all negative. I had had two periods of heavy bleeding. If I *had* been pregnant, I had surely lost the baby. My husband and I hadn't made love for nearly 3 weeks. That is a very long time.

'I've thought about it,' I replied when the nurse returned. She was dressed in blue, holding a clipboard with several patients' names. She looked very distracted. I was sure she had a million things to do. 'I'm definitely not pregnant,' I announced.

'Are you 100% sure?' she asked.

'I'm 99.9% sure. I never say 100%.'

'Okay, follow me.'

In hindsight, I should have asked for a pregnancy test. I should have left the clinic, run across the street where there was a pharmacy and bought one. This would have saved me a lot of pain and guilt. My rational mind (my ego) simply couldn't accept the possibility I might be pregnant. The odds were so slim. Yet I should have admitted I wasn't sure. Fortunately, my son was unharmed by the exams.

If We Don't Attune...

Angels send advice to help us. If we ignore this advice, we prevent them from helping us. I cannot stress how important it is to attune. Pay attention to that funny feeling in your gut or that voice that says, 'Think twice.' How many times have you been driving late at night, when you hear a voice in your head which tells you to stop and rest for a bit? Even if you think this voice is silly, you have nothing to lose if you pull over and rest for half an hour. You'll find the guidance is always sensible. Regret is something none of us want to live with; attuning regularly to the higher voice within and without ensures you do not have to live with poor decisions and the remorse that inevitably comes from them.

Attain

Attaining is the last of the three 'A's. Attaining spirituality is a continual process of attending and attuning. It is never completed and never quite begun. Think of attainment as cycles of growth. As I mentioned, death and birth are vital signs in the soul's journey. The death of a loved one or the birth of a family member symbolize important chapters in a griever's life. They help us understand the infinite exchange of energy. Once one cycle of growth is completed, we embark on a new journey with a new goal and the ultimate aim of realizing our life purpose.

Cycles of Growth

With the tumultuous first 3 months of my pregnancy behind me, I began to settle into a routine. I busied myself decorating my son's room and buying him clothes. It was time for me to enjoy my pregnancy. I was like every expectant mother: full of hopes and fears. Would I be a good mother? Would my son love me? What would he look like? I was preoccupied with the same questions that every pregnant mom wonders about at some point. Week by week, little changes were taking place, not just in my body, but also in my mind. I developed a new-found faith.

Pregnancy realigned me. It encouraged me to confront any remaining grief from losing my mother and brother, ultimately helping me to attain new levels of growth and spirituality. The people we lose serve as markers on our journey to become more spiritual. We can clearly define periods or cycles of growth, viewing the impact a person's death has on our life. If you believe in angels, then you should know you don't have to live without the people we lose. Loved ones who pass on to the other side remain firm fixtures in our life; we just can't see them. In the same way, we can't see air or emotions, but we know they are real events whose impact on our world has clear consequences. Just think of tornadoes or road rage! Angels are all around us. We only need to ask for their help to realize how present they are in our lives.

Attaining and Manifesting Goals

There are many ways to attain goals. Achieving a goal requires hard work and dedication. However, angels can help us attain earthly as well as spiritual goals. They are here to guide us through every change we experience, including the loss of a loved one. Don't believe me? My mother used to say, 'Ask and you shall receive.'

When I was 13 I made two demands in a diary: 1) that I would move away when I was 20; and 2) that I would find the man of my dreams. These events occurred one week before I turned 20. I still have the diary entry scribbled in desperate purple crayon, the writings of a lovesick teenager. It makes me laugh to think how that 13-year-old got her wish 6 years later, when I met my husband-to-be on the train platform thanks to a delayed train. We moved in together shortly after we met, and I never returned home. What 13-year-old has the guts to write demands to the universe? I did, because I believed then and I still believe now. The universe listens. You just need to make yourself heard. I think we can all learn from my 13-year-old self.

God wants your dreams to be realized as long as they come from a sincere place. Sometimes, he even lets us experience destructive events to help us grow as people. So be careful of what you wish for; it may, in fact, come true.

Step 9

Don't Give Up—It's Never Too Late:
Techniques to Encourage Healing

The workshops I've set up have given me the amazing opportunity to interact with women of different ages, faiths and backgrounds. I've learned a lot about myself and others through our discussions about spirituality. One evening a woman in her fifties turned to me and said she envied the fact that I'd found my path so early. I reminded the woman that she shouldn't envy me; if anything I should envy her. This woman had shown great courage in fleeing her country and the laws that prevented freedom of speech. The government recognized only one religion, a religion the woman felt wasn't hers.

I was born in a country that takes freedom for granted. We think it is owed to us. I am not sure I would have shown the courage and determination the woman showed in fleeing her country. Her story taught me a lesson which I will never forget: It's never too late to reconnect with your spirituality. No matter your age, faith or background, spirituality is innate. Our spirituality is as sacred as it is boundless. The only person who can become an obstacle to your growth is *you*. We often use death or other misfortunes as an excuse to deny our spirituality. We are reluctant to confront truth.

Why the Truth Hurts

On earth we don't always want to hear the truth, because truth often leads to change. When I tried to help a friend gain a clearer perspective, I was shocked by the backlash. I lost the friendship as a result of being too honest. People want the truth, but only a small portion. Usually, most people are seeking reassurance. Reassurance allows us to continue with old patterns of behavior without feeling too guilty. There is a time and place for reassurance. However, if we know we are doing something wrong, I believe we shouldn't rely on a friend to assure us that it's okay.

For a long time I relied on friends to tell me it was okay. Even worse, I was the friend that told others it would be okay when I knew full well it wouldn't be. How rare and precious is the friend who has the guts to tell us the truth! Those who are honest with me I keep closest to my heart. It shows they are not afraid to love me in the right way. They are willing to lose me if they cannot help me be a better person. You may think this doesn't make sense; surely a friend who loved you would fight for your friendship. Of course he or she will fight, but if they see that you are making the wrong decision in your life, they shouldn't stand by and support you through these decisions. Sometimes we all need to hear 'no.' It's a very important word to be able to say, especially if you know how and when to say it.

My best friend has stood the test of time, because she always knows when to say no. I have her to thank for the advice she gave me while I tried to conceive. I was stressed out, living the life of two people. She was the one who taught me the importance of the word 'no.' It wasn't easy learning to say no; it took several hospital stays, but once I learned I never forgot. The change in my mind, body and spirit spoke for itself. Don't live your life for other people, forgetting yourself along the way. This is what Mom did. I was not going to burn at both ends of the wick like she did and cut my life short.

Facing the Truth

It's never too late to take your spirituality into your own hands. Each of us has painful memories we'd like to forget, but forgetting our problems rarely solves them. They linger, waiting to flare up the minute we encounter stress. There are many techniques you can use to help you confront deep-rooted issues.

I remind readers that these suggestions are based on personal experience and do not replace consultation with a medical professional.

Techniques to Heal

• **Hypnotherapy**

Hypnotherapy reprograms thinking, replacing old associations with positive ones. Hypnotherapy, if successful, will change certain patterns of behavior or thinking. For traumatic experiences, you might want to consider past-life regression or counseling.

• **Past-Life Regression**

This type of hypnosis isn't for everyone. You don't need to believe in past lives to undergo past-life regression. One hypnotist suggested that I think of past lives as a story or backboard that helps the mind understand certain experiences and trauma. While I believe in past lives, I would not recommend past-life regression to everyone. It helped me end a recurrent nightmare which had caused disturbances in my sleep for years. It can be traumatic reliving experiences. You should only think of undergoing past-life regression if you have a solid support network established of friends, family and professional health providers. I would also recommend counseling before and after a past-life regression session.

• **Counseling**

This is the most traditional form of healing. It may take years for counseling to have an impact on your thinking. It certainly isn't the quickest way to confront deep-rooted issues, but it is by far the most effective and rewarding. Make sure you have a good rapport with your counselor or therapist. It is necessary you feel comfortable and safe in your sessions.

• Peer Workshops and Meditation Circles

Peer workshops and meditation circles offer an alternative to traditional one-to-one sessions. Opt for smaller groups where participation and discussion are encouraged. This will ensure you get the most out of each session. You should check the qualifications of the organizers and teachers before attending. The mission of the group should also be clearly cited on the website or flyer along with contact details. If you are still unsure, ask for a recommendation.

• Self-Education

Books, DVDs and the Internet are all excellent sources of information. However, they are not sufficient alone. Deep-rooted issues need to be confronted in a professional environment with the help of qualified individuals. Weekly progress should be monitored by people who understand your issues and can help you if you experience difficulties. If you are not ready to share your issues, you can read about people with similar experiences. Just remember this is not a solution in itself, but a step among many towards turning grief into guidance.

'To Thine Own Self Be True'

After learning it was okay to say no, something funny happened. I became more interested in my spirituality. I never realized what I was sacrificing in unstable relationships. I sacrificed the best parts of me, trying to help deflect others from hopeless situations.

Did I ever stop to realize *I* was in a hopeless situation? Though I had every reason to be happy, I felt something was missing. I couldn't put a finger on it. I lost some of myself along the way: *I was missing.* My mother always said, 'Where did my sweet girl go?' Life hadn't always been kind to me, but that was no reason to be unkind to others—most of all myself. I had a lot of homework to do. It's true I fell behind in recent years. I wasn't the person I wanted to be. In my 10 years of traveling, I did not learn the most vital lesson: how to be true to myself. Mom said, 'To thine own self be true.' I didn't understand the importance of Shakespeare's words until I became a mother.

In my experience, you can't pretend to be someone you are not when you become a mother. There is nowhere to hide, *literally*. The test comes when you find yourself in a very private room, staring at the most soulful being you have ever seen. This being, your newborn baby, has trusting, gentle eyes that seem to say, 'Teach me, love me. Please show me the way.' How can you do these things if you don't love yourself; if you haven't learned the greatest lessons in your life? This was the question I asked myself when I fell pregnant. I had not listened to the message in the dream. I had put my son at risk. Was I *really* ready for a child, when I was still a child? We all experience tests. They do not always come in the form of a birth or death. They can come in the form of another loss, like job loss. Tests also appear when we believe we are at our best, our strongest point in our career. The spiritual world has a funny way of testing us when we believe we are invincible.

My Journey to Be True

I diligently set to work finding out who I really was. I attended numerous workshops and read every self-help book imaginable. My bookshelves are heaving with self-help books for mothers, writers, anger management, Americans abroad. You name it, I probably have it. They say you can't learn life from books. I disagree. I think you can learn quite a bit. Books frame a person's perspective. No book can give you that elusive answer you seek, but they can point you in the right direction, and with each chapter I read, I was closer to finding the real me. Every week my tummy expanded, so did my faith. I always knew children were a gift, but I never imagined that my abilities would return during pregnancy.

My son was a divine gift which allowed me to regain the spiritual gifts I had lost. I am grateful for my abilities because I use them for the good of my family. I can reach out and connect with the people I love in a way I would never have done previously. Unlike the dream I had in Cornwall, I chose to listen to my mother's messages. I dutifully bought a fan, a monitor and books on breastfeeding in order to minimize the chances of 'cot death': the unexplained condition my brother had. It didn't stop people from trying to give me the same advice all over again. Family, friends and strangers continued to emphasize the importance of these three things. At a certain point, I laughed and told Mom to stop sending me the message. I got it the first time.

I knew I needed her help, but I never imagined how difficult the last few weeks of pregnancy would be for me or that my son would be born 5 weeks early. There was a reason for the constant contact: I was about to be hospitalized. I just didn't know it. There were warning signs, but I didn't want to slow down and listen to my intuition. Once again I risked something precious. This time it wasn't my son. It was me. My life was at risk.

Step 10

Trust Your Intuition: *Exercises to Increase Intuition*

A Step Too Far

Climbing the stairs to Montmartre, I knew I was taking a step too far. I chose to ignore my intuition, which told me I was in trouble.

I was 26 weeks pregnant and my belly bounced side to side as I climbed what must have been the 200th step. 'Are you sure this is a good idea?' my husband asked doubtfully. He frowned deeply.

I stood on the step below him, a little out of breath, smiling like the Cheshire Cat from *Alice in Wonderland*. I ignored his question and the little voice at the back of my head that told me to slow down.

We finally reached the top. The view was truly breathtaking. Paris was spread below us, a sea of soft shades of grey, the Eiffel Tower rising above the tide, triumphant. Its lights twinkled in the distance. The sun began to set. Patches of golden light broke through the winter sky. It could have been a painting. The windswept leafless winter trees, the street performers, the artists and musicians congregated outside the church. Everything was beautiful to my enthusiastic eye. I was on a hormone high, in the second trimester of my pregnancy. Trouble was, I didn't know it. I thought it was perfectly normal to have the urge to climb 300 steps to see Montmartre or take the train to the other side of town to see the Musée d'Orsay.

My husband and I dined, toured the city, laughed and held hands. It was great until I got back to England and reality sank in. I lay in bed writhing in pain; my hip killed me. I felt terrible.

'What's wrong with you?' my husband asked. His voice was tinged with a mixture of worry and frustration. The latter because he knew I had overdone it in Paris, the former because I was pregnant with his son. 'Do you want me to stay here with you?'

'No, go to Las Vegas,' I grumbled. I was looking forward to a little time alone.

I should have made him stay. Something was telling me to ask him to stay, but he was going for work and I didn't want to disrupt his schedule. A few hours after my husband left for the airport, the pain got so bad I decided I needed to take action.

An Unpleasant Surprise

The doctor wanted to see me right away. I made my way to the other room, where my doctor sat at her desk studying my notes. She asked me to undress. When I did, I was surprised to find my leg swollen and turning a light purple.

'This isn't related to your pre-existing injury,' she pronounced grimly. I looked down at my leg and nodded. 'I am fairly sure you have a blood clot in your leg,' she said, wasting no time.

I was shocked by this diagnosis. After all, my mother had passed away 3 years before from an aneurysm, the consequence of a blood clot in her leg.

In the space of 5 minutes my doctor ordered a scan and an ultrasound of my leg. She also made a request for the maternity ward to accept me as a patient. I resigned myself to the thought that I would be in hospital for quite a long time as I was sent to the ultrasound screening area.

'See that dark formation?' the training nurse asked the trainee.

'On the left vein?'

'That's right. We think it's a DVT, a deep vein thrombosis.'

'Is that bad?' I asked, interrupting the training session.

'We need a third opinion, but from the looks of it I think you'll need to be admitted and stay in the hospital at least three days,' the nurse said, trying to keep a blank and impartial face. I could see she was affected by the sight of a heavily pregnant woman in such a vulnerable state.

The doctor on call came in to study the images. 'Yes, the diagnosis is correct,' she confirmed. 'It is without a doubt a DVT.' I asked the doctor what a DVT was. She explained it was a blood clot in one of my deep veins.

'Is it dangerous?' I asked, knowing full well it was. She nodded sympathetically and told me that if the clot broke off and moved to my lungs, it could give me a pulmonary embolism, which could be potentially life-threatening.

I arrived on the maternity ward exhausted. After 30 minutes, the nurses cleared a bed for me. I lay in the bed feeling emotional, but relieved that the staff had admitted me to the ward. The doctors would monitor me and ensure my condition did not deteriorate. I made a few desperate phone calls on my mobile. I explained to my mother-in-law what had happened, in broken Italian. She understood and said she would take the first flight. I will always remain eternally grateful for the support she gave me. She acted like a second mother to me in that painful moment of need. My husband also took the first flight from Vegas. It was an exhausting, emotionally taxing experience for all of us.

Learning to Trust Intuition

If I had trusted my intuition, the situation might have turned out differently. Sometimes we are given the means to prevent certain events from happening. The angels send us signs; whether or not we choose to listen to their guidance is our choice. Again, grief and other emotions like anger or even stubbornness can prevent us from listening to this guidance. So it is important you take the steps to heal properly before you can receive guidance.

In Step 9: Don't Give Up—It's Never Too Late, I listed techniques for healing. Please refer again to this chapter if you think you might need extra time to heal. I have spent a lifetime discussing my pain and making an active effort to heal. I think it is this earnest self-assessment which has opened me to guidance and ultimately helped me grow spiritually.

Learning to discuss pain in a positive and proactive manner is not an easy task. You may come from a culture or family which discourages talking. Try to find a group of supportive people or a qualified individual to help you discuss your feelings little by little. Perspective can open you to guidance. By trusting your intuition and feelings, you will ultimately form a deeper connection with your divine purpose.

Techniques for Increasing Intuition

Intuition plays a vital role in decision-making. Some refer to it as a 'gut feeling.' You cannot make an informed decision without listening to your intuition. Think of it as an instinct. Intuition provides us with an innate understanding of a situation before we have time to fully process the facts.

Intuition is life's invisible melody. The more we listen, the more we can begin to recognize the rise and fall of its beat. When we effectively tune in to our intuition, we understand our life's unique rhythm and the rhythm of those around us. When the rhythm is off, we can spot it in the subtle nuances of a friend's expression, a phone call, or a suspicious feeling about a stranger crossing the road. There are a number of exercises you can use to increase your intuition and start tuning in to life's invisible melody.

• Partner Exercises
Ask a friend or relative to help you train your intuition by visualizing or thinking about their favorite color. You need to be in a quiet room and totally relaxed. It might help if the friend holds a card with the word or color. You shouldn't be able to see the card, but it will help your partner accurately visualize the color. Concentrate on the word or color that appears in your mind after a few minutes of silence. You can also use cards with numbers.

Numbers may be easier for you to visualize intuitively. Make sure your partner and you switch sides throughout the exercise.

Note: Even if you don't get any of the cards right, you are opening your mind to intuitive thinking. However, please ensure you feel comfortable with your partner; you shouldn't feel competitive or nervous. Your mind should be calm and focused.

• Other Techniques

A common technique many people use when developing their intuition is to think of a friend you haven't spoken to in a while. Make sure the friend is someone you regularly have contact with. The more you think of this person, the more you attract their attention. Look at photos, letters or emails. Concentrate on your desire for your friend to make contact. It should be a positive, uplifting desire.

Don't be surprised if you receive a phone call or email. Your friend may say, 'I was just thinking of you.' If it doesn't immediately work, don't get disheartened; try again with another friend who may be more in tune with your thoughts. If you find the exercise difficult, ask the angels for a helping hand. Consider meditating before attempting the exercise again.

Note: When you successfully complete the exercise, ask a friend or relative to pick someone in your circle of friends. This secret person should think of you until you make contact. This second part of the exercise might be harder to complete. You may not have a group of friends interested in developing their intuition. If this is the case, consider joining development circles (discussed below).

• Development Circles

If you are serious about increasing your intuition, consider enrolling in workshops with qualified teachers. Be careful which course you choose as these kinds of workshops can be unregulated, ineffective and unsafe. Ask a friend who has already attended a course or someone who is an established authority on the subject to recommend a development circle.

• Get Reading!
There is so much material available on the subject of increasing intuition. There are a number of books I could recommend, but this is a highly personal matter. Go to a specialist bookstore or browse online for titles that capture your interest. Dreams and meditation are also wonderful ways to increase intuition. While there are general books on the subject of increasing intuition, there are also very specific books on how to increase intuition in dreams and through meditation. Again, a gut feeling is a very good indication if the book and its techniques will be effective for you.

A Prayer
Recovery was slow after doctors discovered the DVT in my left leg. Luckily, the clot did not break off or travel. Doctors worked hard to thin my blood and reduce the risk of the clot traveling. I prayed to Mother Mary constantly to protect my unborn son. When I prayed to Mary, I felt compassion and peace. I was protected and I knew everything would be okay. Mary lost a son. She sacrificed a life's work and love for a higher purpose. This theme was familiar to me as I suffered a similar loss. I didn't want to experience what my mother felt when she lost my brother. I needed all the help I could get. I vowed to Mary that if she helped me, I would help her spread love and faith whenever I could. I had a duty to keep this promise. I didn't know that in a matter of days I would hear her call.

Mary's Call
The first night back, I had trouble falling asleep. I kept the lights on, something I do when I am tired or feeling tense. It didn't help. I still felt lonely and separated from my family who were sleeping upstairs. I was confined to sleeping on the daybed

downstairs.

That night, I had the strangest dream. I dreamed I was in my mother's ex-best friend's house. I had not seen my mother's ex-best friend in 15 years; that was a very long time, more than half my life. There was no reason to dream of her. There was nothing I said or did throughout the day that could have triggered the dream. Yet when I woke up I was gripped by the strangest sensation. The dream was real. It wasn't a dream, but a message. The dream came back to me in phases. I closed my eyes and tried to remember the scenes.

I recalled walking around my mother's ex-best friend's house. The house was dark. The lights were on and it was daytime, but there was a heaviness which clung to the walls. People were dressed in black. I realized the heaviness was grief. Someone had died. I immediately assumed it was my mother's ex-best friend's husband. I knew him growing up. It was logical I might dream of him. We had spent many summers together. Yet something didn't make sense. My mother's ex-best friend wasn't crying as one would expect her to if she had lost her husband. Her grief was much softer. I couldn't understand who had died.

I remember this frustrated me in the dream. No one could see me at the funeral. I was an invisible witness as if I were viewing a mystery. Suddenly, an old man appeared and led me through the rooms of the house. It was all so surreal. He kept telling me he knew where his glasses were. He repeated the fact over and over. He told me he had passed away and wanted to give his daughter this message. I was a little startled in the dream, but I dutifully listened. He showed me the drawer where he kept his glasses. It was a wooden drawer of an old oak desk upstairs. There was a light on the desk, glowing in the early evening light. The drawer was full of pairs of antique glasses. 'You must tell my daughter I know where my glasses are. They are in the drawer upstairs.' He repeated the message a hundred times. I don't remember the rest of the dream.

When I woke up, I had the nagging feeling that the dream must be a message for my mother's ex-best friend, but I was confused. Who was the old man in the dream? I couldn't remember if my mother's ex-best friend had ever spoken of her father. Why on earth would her father harp on the subject of his glasses? How peculiar! The glasses must hold some secret significance. There must be a way I could find out. I logged on to my computer and googled 'obituaries' and my mother's ex-best friend's last name.

My heart nearly stopped when I read that just ten days earlier, her father had passed away. There was an announcement in the local *Times*. This is customary in America, especially in the Deep South. You make an announcement in the paper with a brief summary of the person's life and their surviving family. I skimmed over the announcement. My nervous eye did not linger. Somehow I had accessed a private communication between a father and a daughter.

I shut my laptop. It wasn't a coincidence. The timing of the dream and her father's passing was too connected for me to ignore. *Now what?* I thought as I hobbled to the kitchen to make breakfast. It was six in the morning. The birds chirped away in the garden oblivious to my dilemma. Their happy song annoyed me. What was I supposed to do? I found myself in the awkward position of being messenger. There's a reason people say, 'Don't shoot the messenger.' I didn't want to be the bystander who bore the fury of the person receiving the message. I knew that my mother's ex-best friend might not appreciate my efforts to help her, especially after everything that had happened between my mother and her. I longed to control the outcome of the situation. A thousand questions raced through my mind.

Who or what force was behind this dream? Did my mother want me to help her ex-best friend in some gesture of compassion or was this part of the promise I had made in the hospital, when I prayed to Mother Mary to protect my son? I promised I would spread love and faith. The love and faith between a child and parent is one of the strongest bonds we experience. This message might hold the key to strengthening the bond between a father and daughter. I had found peace in my mother's messages; who was I to deny another person a chance to do the same, even if that person had hurt my mother?

Delivering the Message

With Dad's help I passed on the message to my mother's ex-best friend. Later, Dad ran into her daughter at the library. She said her mother felt much more at 'peace' about the death. She explained that her grandfather had suffered from dementia in the last years of his life. The fact that her grandfather mentioned the location of his glasses in the dream was proof his memory was restored. By remembering the location of his glasses he assured both his daughter and granddaughter that he knew what had happened to him. My mother's ex-best friend was afraid her father wouldn't realize he had died. It was nice to be able to reassure them that their loved one was fine.

I was given the opportunity to pass on a message of love. I hoped I honored the angels' faith in me. It's not easy being a messenger. Luckily, I haven't received any other messages apart from the odd piece of advice from my mother. We are all capable of receiving messages, but to act as a messenger one must earn the right to work with the angels. I do not feel I earned this privilege. It takes dedication and hard work.

If You Receive a Message...

Receiving and interpreting divine messages is not easy. It's not a path I would recommend readily to others. The responsibility is enormous. However, if you find you are constantly receiving information about others that later comes true or would have helped them in the moment, this might be a sign that you should be working with the angels.

The path of a messenger is never easy. It can be a very lonely path, but it can also be a very fulfilling one. Free will does play a big role in how one fulfills this path. Intention and belief are key components in delivering divine messages to others. When I helped my mother's ex-best friend I had the intention of fulfilling my promise to Mother Mary, so I was in a very good place to deliver the message.

Development and training are crucial if you want to help others with angelic messages. The responsibility is as serious as a doctor's or therapist's responsibility in caring and protecting for patients.

A Message to Readers

I hope my experiences show that when people, even skeptics, open themselves up to the possibility of coincidences, they will realize that synchronicity plays a crucial role in each of our lives. The more we pay attention to the meaningful coincidences that occur around us, the more we can learn about the hidden nature of our mind, body and spirit.

Step 11

Practice Appreciation: *The Importance of Mindfulness in Our Lives*

This is the final step on your journey to turn grief into guidance. Appreciation encourages spiritual growth. When we pause to consider our blessings, especially after the loss of a loved one, we gain perspective. Perspective navigates us through uncharted waters, ultimately deciding our course. Practicing appreciation daily will help focus your energy towards accomplishing a goal or facing a specific challenge. This is so important after experiencing the loss of a close friend or family member. We often find it difficult to confront situations without the physical presence and assurance of a loved one.

Think of appreciation as one way of boosting your spiritual self-confidence. Look around and start noting how many positive things and people you have in your life. Appreciation is one step towards your life purpose. Every day you practice appreciation, you get closer to realizing that purpose. Appreciation isn't just about gratitude; it is also about savoring the moment.

Ways to Practice Appreciation

• Prayers of Thanks

Saying prayers of thanks or counting blessings helps order thoughts. If you are prone to worrying before you fall asleep, this will focus attention on appreciation versus anxiety. Food, a warm bed, a loving partner are simple pleasures we often take for granted. Count every blessing, even the smallest; this will deepen and prolong your appreciation, ensuring you live more richly.

• Make a List

Writing our blessings down helps us realize how fortunate we truly are. If you are going through a difficult period, take time out to write down your blessings every day. Make a comprehensive list and place it on a wall or desk, so you can look at the list often throughout the day. You will be surprised how quickly negative thinking is replaced with positive affirmations.

• Record the Moment

Make hard copies of digital photos. Seeing your life in pictures allows us to relive our happiest moments. Capture the moment and the feeling. People have the tendency to remember the negative events of their life over the positive ones. This distorts thinking and prevents deeper levels of appreciation. Video recordings or voice recordings are also good ways to record the moment.

• Thank Loved Ones

Often we forget to thank those closest to us for their support. Expressing gratitude to friends and family promotes appreciation in our relationships. Once appreciation is expressed, it is often reciprocated, deepening a connection. If you find yourself wishing you had thanked your loved one more before they died, it's never too late to write them a letter. They will hear and feel your appreciation with the help of angels.

Appreciating the Journey

Nothing compared to the moment my son was born, not even the day I married my husband. Finally, the hole Mom had left in my life was beginning to heal. Nothing would replace Mom, but at least there was new life in the valley. Winter passed and the first blooms of spring could be seen shooting out of the ground. April 2011 was one of the warmest and most beautiful months on record in the UK. The British were busy preparing for the Royal Wedding. The mood was jubilant. I couldn't have been happier. I finally had the family for which I had prayed. I had finally given birth to my son, albeit 5 weeks prematurely. I said my prayers in the early hours of the 28th before shutting my eyes. Mainly, I prayed for my son and his health, and thanked God for the wonderful staff at the hospital.

Becoming a mother was a journey in itself. The only way I could negotiate the rough terrain was by learning to sit back, relinquish control and enjoy the ride. It took 2 long weeks for my son to leave the hospital. Every day, I made the hour-and-a-half trip to see him on the neonatal ward. I was exhausted. Instead of being elated, I was emotionally drained. My son was not at home, resting with me. He was in an incubator on the other side of town. Though I was grateful that he was surrounded by a wonderful team of doctors and nurses, I just wished he could come home with his parents like any newborn.

Dad came to visit all the way from America, which was a happy distraction. It didn't matter that his grandson was in a neonatal ward; he looked just like any proud grandfather. After what seemed like an eternity, the doctors were ready to release my son from the hospital. It was the moment we had waited for; our son was finally coming home and my father was there to witness the moment.

We were like any first-time parents. We weren't sure how the car seat worked. He looked so tiny in the colossal seat. Was he sitting right? Was he comfortable? Too many questions; Dad didn't have time to reassure us. My husband and I ran around like Tweedle Dum and Tweedle Dee. It took an hour and a half to get home. We stopped along the way and fed our son. He threw up, probably from the pressure of being propped up by the car seat. His spine was very weak. This threw us into sheer panic. What were we doing wrong? We got home and placed him in his cot. He didn't like that. He screamed and screamed. He was used to the bright lights of the ward and his clear plastic bed. Nothing we did settled him. Finally, he managed to fall asleep. It was all so new to us. If we thought we were exhausted before, we were delirious now.

Life had come full circle. I was the mother and protector now. It was easy to think I was alone and everything fell on my shoulders. As much as dads want to help, they can't in the first few hours and weeks of becoming a parent. They just don't have the anatomy to help. As wonderful as it is to become a mother, it can also be a very scary and lonely time; especially if you have lost your own mother. Though my mother wasn't around to help me, this didn't mean she wasn't looking out for me. I had a platoon of angels helping me. I just couldn't see them.

The past 18 months have taught me anything is possible. Faith and spirituality are as mysterious and infinite as time. Most of us think time is linear, but I prefer to think it is circular, starting with the family. Time encompasses so many things, perspective and memory, but most of all it holds the key to our existence and the love we feel for each other. Though time marches on, our love for those in our life and those we have lost is constant. A message now and then, again, is all I need to reaffirm my faith.

Practicing Appreciation

I wish I could say I appreciated every moment of the first few days and weeks of my son's life. Unfortunately, I'd be lying. I was consumed with worry. I didn't pause often enough to consider the miracle of life or the mystery of creation. I was too caught up in the worries common to new mothers. But I've never stopped praying or counting my blessings. When I shut my eyes and concentrated on the image of my son, I felt a deep gratitude flood my senses. Eventually, I found ways to prolong this feeling throughout the day, thanking loved ones for their help and recording the moment in pictures and scrapbooks. Appreciation doesn't always come naturally. It is something we learn with mindfulness.

Techniques to Encourage Mindfulness

In a way, appreciation is like an active meditation. Practicing appreciation involves focusing your mental energies throughout the day. Often people ask, 'Are you a glass half full or half empty kind of person?' In my mind, the glass is neither half full nor empty; it simply is. To truly appreciate what we have, we need to accept and understand all aspects of our life: good and bad. To label the glass as half full or half empty is to negotiate the value of the glass and its contents.

This comes back to judgment. As humans, it is very hard to supersede judgment. It is one of the most basic and innate instincts we possess. It is linked to fear and animal survival instincts. Practicing appreciation is about embracing and loving the positive aspects of our life as well as the negative. Most of the techniques I listed earlier in this chapter involve focusing mostly on positive aspects; this is because grief can be a very negative and isolating experience for many people.

To counterbalance this experience, it is necessary to focus on the positive aspects of the griever's life. However, I'd like to point out that true appreciation is blind. To really appreciate life, one has to embrace both the positive and negative aspects in order to learn and grow spiritually. This is true of loss as well. When we lose a loved one it may feel like the end of the world, but it is also an opportunity to begin a new world.

As you've learned from the previous ten steps, our loved ones are here to guide and protect us with the help of angels. We are always surrounded by the light of their love and their presence. I call it a 'Circle of Light.' You only have to be mindful of this circle to appreciate its symmetry with our lives. Here are a few tips to encourage mindfulness:

• Monitor Stress Levels

The more stressed we are, the less mindful we become. It's a relationship of reciprocals. Monitor your stress levels throughout the day. When you are feeling particularly stressed, take time out and remove yourself from the situation which is causing stress.

• Lifestyle Choices

While stress is increasingly thought of as a modern disease, I believe it is a lifestyle choice which can be controlled with well thought-out decisions about the kind of lifestyle we want to live. For instance, don't leave your phone near your bed at night and make sure to switch smartphones which receive emails and social feeds off at night. Make a rule not to check work emails after 7pm. These are sensible lifestyle choices which will make a big difference in managing stress levels and freeing up mental space. Similarly, if you always find yourself helping or doing things for others and feeling resentful, learn how to set boundaries and say no!

• Birds of a Feather Flock Together

You know the old saying? Well, it's true. Be careful of the company you keep. We may not be able to choose our family, but we can choose our friends. Friends' beliefs and behavior have a profound effect on our life. If you are surrounded by stressed friends who have no desire to change their lives, you will quickly find yourself in a similar rut. Take a spiritual inventory of the people in your life. You don't need to cut people out of your life, but maybe slowly reduce the time you spend with friends who are permanently stressed, especially if you leave their company feeling tired, drained or negative. Invite friends to join you in your quest to be more mindful. If they show interest, use stress as a positive way to bond.

• Be Careful of the Judgments You Make

This advice comes from a wise friend who is deeply involved in meditation and mindfulness. She had a life-changing experience with someone who lived on the streets. Though she is a very open person, she realized a lot of her ideas about homeless people were largely based on stereotypes. Once she took the time to speak to a homeless person, she was fascinated to learn a new truth, not only about the homeless, but also about herself. Judgments play a big role in our life. Our judgments about others reveal important truths about the way we think and who we are as people. If you find yourself judging someone harshly, ask yourself where this thought originates. Is it a belief you were taught or is it something you assimilated over the years? Try to use your judgments as a spiritual mirror. The more we look at ourselves and our relationships, the more mindful we become and the more deeply we appreciate.

• Connect

When is the last time you truly took time to connect to the people in your life? If we do not make a special effort to connect to loved ones and dig deep, we miss a special opportunity to connect. The more mindful we are of the special people in our lives, the deeper our appreciation and involvement. This involvement is always returned to us with special insight or a loving embrace. Get off-script and ask, 'What is the one thing you want to do before you die?' It might throw your friend or family member at first, but you'll be surprised by the meaningful conversation which will ensue.

The End of a Journey: *Finding Purpose*

After a few weeks of being new parents, my husband and I got to know our son. We formed a real connection and quickly learned his likes and dislikes. I was surprised when our son had colic and let out piercing cries at 3am. We both cried the hours away until dawn. I could feel Mom near me. Something was telling me it was the way I breastfed and the consistency of the milk. I changed my technique and I am happy to report my son never suffered from colic again. Listening to my intuition saved me many unhappy hours with a crying baby. I am glad Mom was around to help me figure things out. I missed her, but it was comforting to know she was watching and helping out when she could.

Like my son, I was growing in my own way. I finally learned to listen to my intuition, turning what could have been grief in a difficult moment into guidance. It would have been all too easy to feel sorry for myself at 3am. So many new mothers have the help of their mothers. Though I was alone in a big city, I chose to focus on the positive. I had the loving support of my husband's family. The past months had taught me that I was not only greatly loved, but also very much guided. There was no reason to feel alone, when I was surrounded with light.

Weeks turned into months and suddenly our baby boy reached a milestone: 6 months. My boy grew more independent by the day. Suddenly he occupied himself and played alone for hours at a time. He didn't need me as much as he did in the first weeks of his life. It feels good to be needed. The minute someone stops needing us it hurts a little, even if it is a relief in the long run. No mother wants to be changing nappies (or diapers) the rest of her life! I didn't know it, but I was at another crossroad.

A Spiritual Crossroad

'What are you going to do when our son doesn't need you as much?' my husband asked. It was a question I had thought about a lot.

'I don't know,' I admitted.

'Well, I think you should decide if you want to try to go back to work,' he said. 'It's a decision every woman faces. I want you to know I'm happy either way as long as *you* are happy.'

I quickly changed the subject, avoiding a lengthy discussion.

A few days later I was still thinking of the conversation. The weather had turned grey and cold. Winter seems interminably long in Britain due to the rainy weather. I fixed my mind on the reward of a coffee. It was a slow morning and now I found myself standing in a long line for a coffee at our local café. I supposed I wasn't the only one in need of a coffee. My son was fussing in his pram. The regulars, the coffee addicts, started to get agitated. We were both tired and emotional. I quickly paid for the coffee and left the café.

I stopped in the middle of the street and began to dab some coffee that had spilled onto my jacket. I noticed a blonde woman at the end of the street. She looked lost. Usually, I am the first person to help a stranger. People always ask me for directions. I must have a friendly face. I am sure my face didn't look friendly that day. Frankly, I was annoyed. The coffee was supposed to be my reward. I wasn't really in the mood to help. I was too concerned with the coffee stains on my jacket. The blonde woman walked towards me. I avoided eye contact. This didn't seem to deter her. I noticed she was carrying a large thin black case. It looked like a portfolio.

'Excuse me, do you live locally?' she asked. I looked up long enough to make eye contact with her. She was quite pretty. She must have been in her late twenties. She had very clear blue eyes, but there was a peculiar look in them. It looked as if she were about to cry. I am a sucker for tears. If I see someone cry, I am likely to well-up too. I was already feeling emotional and now a lost stranger stood in front of me imploring me to help. I couldn't turn her away or lie. I had no choice but to help.

'Yes, I live here,' I grumbled.

'Do you know where I can find the 101 bus to East Ham? I'm going to meet my aunt. She lives on Langham Road.'

I recognized the name of the road instantly. 'You can catch the 101 just across the street,' I said, pointing to a bus stop on the other side of the road. The woman didn't reply. Instead, she just stared blankly at the other end of the street. 'Why don't you call your aunt to make sure it's the right bus stop?' I suggested, not knowing what to say. I didn't want to leave the woman standing on the corner alone.

She got her phone out and dialled her aunt. 'She's going to be so mad. My aunt's at work and can't pick up the phone,' she explained.

I got the feeling the woman's aunt wasn't the nicest person in the world. When her aunt did pick up, it was the briefest of conversations. I thought I could hear scolding on the other end of the phone, but I couldn't be certain. The young blonde woman looked mildly embarrassed as she hung up.

Not knowing what to do, I offered to walk the woman to the stop, as it was on my way home. I asked her if she was an artist.

'Can you speak up? I'm deaf in this ear,' she explained.

I repeated my question. The woman confirmed she was an artist, interviewing at the local high school for a teaching position. I guessed from the teary look in her eye that the interview hadn't gone so well.

'Has it been one of *those* days?' I asked.

'Sorry?'

'It looks like your interview was tough,' I said, eyeing her portfolio. The case looked shiny and new. My heart went out to this young woman. I wondered if she had bought the portfolio in anticipation of the interview.

'Oh, it was awful. There were twelve other candidates and each of us gave a lesson in front of a board of teachers and a classroom of children.'

'That does sound awful. I can't believe they would put so much pressure on the candidates being interviewed.'

'Yes, and I'm not sure how I did.'

'I'm sure you did well. My mother was an art teacher. It's not the easiest job,' I added.

She nodded. Before she could reply, I interrupted: 'We need to cross the road to get to the bus stop. This is the safest place to cross.' The road was a very busy street.

'You don't have to cross the road with me.'

'Don't worry, it's no trouble. It's on my way home anyway.'

I felt compelled to escort the woman to the bus stop. I even made sure the bus stopped near her aunt's house. I was afraid something bad might happen to the woman. She looked distraught as though she didn't have a friend in the world. I wondered if she hadn't performed well in the interview because she couldn't hear the questions properly. Auditoriums often have poor acoustics.

'Thank you. You've really gone above and beyond the call of duty,' she said as I waved goodbye to her.

'You looked like you had a bad day. I know what it feels like to have a bad day,' I replied with a smile.

She nodded and stifled a sob. 'You've been very kind. I really appreciate it. Thank you and Merry Christmas,' she said, before she disappeared out of sight.

I walked home, thinking over the entire experience. The woman had said the oddest thing to me: *'You have gone above and beyond the call of duty.'* These words rattled around my thoughts. Slowly the little cogs in my head churned into life. I was unsure whether it was the coffee or the timing of my encounter. But just as I was wallowing in self-pity, the universe had sent me a very pretty, partially deaf art teacher. Her words and subtle manner stayed with me for the rest of the day. I thought over our conversation several times.

Had the woman been treated badly throughout her life? Had she been bullied for being partially deaf?

From her tearful expression I guessed she had. How sad and how cruel human beings can be to one another! She spoke of a call to duty. I struggled with the meaning behind this expression. I was familiar with the idea of being called or compelled to do something. I was a person who relied on my faith and spirituality to make a lot of my decisions.

Initially, I didn't feel like helping the woman. Perhaps she sensed my reluctance and thought I outdid myself, but she didn't know I enjoyed helping people. It was something from which I derived a lot of pleasure and satisfaction. She had no way of knowing this.

She could only judge my character on my outward appearance. I supposed my appearance was anything but welcoming the moment she decided to talk to me. Still, if I appeared annoyed, why did she decide to ask me for directions? I think it was because I had a stroller with me. I was clearly a mother and a local. Helping the woman was not a call of duty; it was a natural inclination. It was something that came from the heart, compelling me to go out of my way.

Finding Purpose

Here was the answer to my husband's question, 'What are you going to do when our son doesn't need you as much?' There were other people who needed me in small and big ways. God had given me many talents. I had to use them. Something Dad urged me to do, when he said, 'Darling, it's simple. It's in the Bible. God wants you to use the talents he gave you.' Though Dad is not religious, he is highly spiritual. He has read many sacred texts, but the Bible is still one of his favorites for its simple, stoic advice. My father was right. When he said the universe wanted me to use my talents, this struck a deep chord. It woke me up from the inertia of fear, renewing my sense of direction and purpose. I was still afraid, like the servant in the Parable of the Talents (The New American Standard Bible, Matthew 25:14–30; Luke 19:12–27).

The meaning of the parable is clear. Those who do not use their talents live unfulfilled lives and eventually lose the gifts bestowed on them. Those who fearlessly pursue their talents are rewarded in due time with more talents. I had so many opportunities over the years. I certainly never squandered these opportunities. I just never capitalized on them. Another person would have made more out of the opportunities that were given to me. When serious contacts urged me to write a book, I disregarded their offers to help me as a mere show of politeness.

I never considered I had a voice. The Parable of the Talents introduces the passage with the simple advice, 'Be on the alert then, for you do not know the day nor the hour' (Matthew 25:13). I don't know if I was alert or what I like to refer to as 'mindfully awake' that day standing outside the café, dabbing coffee off my sleeve. I think I was annoyed, but I recognized the importance of helping the woman in that crucial moment. I was being tested. I didn't know it at the time. I followed my heart's instinct to help the woman. I sensed she was emotional and lost. I don't think I would ever have turned her away, but it scares me to think I might have been distracted and not seen her.

The woman's suffering highlighted my ineptness. I was wasting time, consumed with drinking coffee; selfish rewards for a self-gratifying lifestyle. We all are guilty of falling victim to the inertia of consumption or stress. The woman's clear blue eyes shook my soul out of its deep slumber. I felt compelled to rise out of the inertia which had gripped me hours earlier. I was inspired to make a real and lasting connection. Yes, I would never see the woman again, but I think we both left knowing we had changed each other's life in some small but very meaningful way.

I felt empowered and she felt relieved. I took some of the burden off her back and showed her that people do care. I am sure she was treated badly during her interview and to be considered even for a moment renewed her faith in herself and others that day. God bless that woman. I hope she got a job at a school that recognized her talent.

There is nothing worse than not having your talent recognized, but as with everything there is always a reason behind our suffering. I truly believe God or the universe does not let us suffer needlessly. I will always remember the woman I encountered for the lesson of humility she taught me. She showed me the meaning of appreciation. You wouldn't think a stranger could teach you so much about yourself. Perhaps she was an angel. I think it is more likely that it was a fated meeting. Thankfully, I recognized the importance of the moment just as I did the day I met my husband on the train platform. It's easy to fail the tests the higher power sends us and ignore the angels' efforts to help us realize our divine purpose.

It was my husband's simple question that finally got me brooding over my real purpose. I wanted to write a book that would help others and bring a message of hope. I wanted to inspire people to live their lives more fully. I know what it feels like to lose someone and not know what to do with the pieces of your life. Yes, grief is shattering, debilitating, but once you pick yourself up you begin to see the light. Grief becomes a tool to rebuild your life and find guidance.

When Mom asked when I was going to write my book in the reading at the SAGB, I didn't really understand what she meant. I had written many books. I was a writer. I once lamented to a journal that I would go 'mad' if I didn't write down my thoughts. I still feel this way, but it is clear to me that this was the real talent I couldn't live without. It was the talent that was going to squeeze the passion out of my life if I didn't give it free rein and make the most of my opportunities.

How to Find Your Purpose

Now that you've learned to transform grief into guidance, having completed your own journey, examine your life carefully. Do you have a burning desire to do something? Does the thought of not being able to achieve your dream make you sick at night? Pay attention to this feeling. It's a gentle warning that you need to listen to your instincts and honor the talents God gave you.

Think back to your earliest passion. Maybe you wanted to be a musician, a teacher or a nurse. Children are less inhibited than adults. As we grow, our inhibitions prevent us from achieving our deepest desires. I am not suggesting you drop your career and family to become a nurse at the age of 55. You don't need to throw your present life away for the sake of a dream; consider volunteering or donating to a charity that helps train nurses. However, if you are bent on achieving a dream you've had since you were little, make realistic plans that accommodate your commitments. Speak to friends and family before you invest energy, time and hard-earned resources. Every dream is achievable, but the best dreams are the ones we share with the people we love.

Healing Family

With this chapter, we near the end of the 11 steps. The spiritual process to turn grief into guidance is never complete, much like our soul's journey. When we finish one cycle, we embark on a new journey to understand our soul's ever-evolving purpose. This journey is not limited to loss. It can manifest in many different forms: a birth, a move to another city or country, a divorce, a new job or family holiday. The possibility for lessons is limitless.

Throughout our lives we encounter many spiritual crossroads. The loss of a loved one, partner, parent or child represents one of the biggest challenges we face in our relatively short lives. How we react to the absence of that person is a very big indication of the legacy we wish to leave.

Our lives are a message. Our lifestyle choices greatly affect our surviving friends and family. It is all too easy to let grief destroy deep family bonds. One might think that death unites people, but often it tears families apart as they grapple with the many complex emotions death can stir up. Jealousy, sibling rivalry, mistrust, old family feuds often float to the surface in trying times. As people negotiate pain, this pain spreads, becoming a collective scar which is felt by future generations.

Sometimes pain can be a healing experience for the surviving family, a cleansing. This is rare. When my mother died, I think my father and I grew closer because our family was so small. I had no siblings. I believe the communication between my father and me was more effective because it was just the two of us. One to one, we could discuss delicate topics in a controlled environment.

My son and husband were absent from these emotional conversations. If they had been involved, I think we might not have experienced several of the 'breakthrough' moments Dad and I experienced in our relationship. We would have been more guarded with each other. The bigger a family is, the harder it is to reach out to each family member and connect. This shouldn't discourage surviving family. However, I think acceptance of human nature plays an important role in how we confront the challenges of a funeral, inheritance and dividing a loved one's property.

When my grandfather died, it was strange to see what had been a previously united family of three brothers and a surviving wife fall apart. My grandfather and his eccentricities had held our family together. We didn't realize it at the time, but his absence was a deep loss. When his wife, my grandmother, passed away, the pain was revisited. The scar ran deeper as old hurt re-emerged. It has lessened over the years, but it can still be felt. Our family has never gathered in the same house since my grandfather passed away. I think this is a testament alone to how a death can change family dynamics. Begging the question: How can we heal collective pain? This is a very difficult and delicate topic. There is no easy answer. As much as it is hard to admit, many of our family members do not want to take responsibility for their actions. They do not want to heal.

As much as we reach out to them, the contact proves ineffective and may even worsen an already strained situation. This is when free will comes into play. While we have a responsibility to help others, our greatest spiritual responsibility is to help ourselves first. If we cannot heal, how can we expect to help others? Undoubtedly people begin with good intentions of helping others, but these intentions are rarely realized if a person has not worked to understand the events and course of his life. His confusion is transferred to others and conversations become entangled; history repeats itself. Sometimes a situation is so tense that any involvement can only result in a worsening of ties.

So how can we avoid getting on the family merry-go-round? As much as we love our family members, the loss of a loved one can increase existing tension and misunderstandings. Most of my book is about an individual journey to heal. However, every journey intersects with another person's quest. Pain is often multigenerational. When we discuss healing of the individual, we must also acknowledge the role families play in this process. Thus, this book would not be complete without a final chapter to address the complex topic of family and how we negotiate the physical, emotional and spiritual loss of a loved one with surviving friends and family members.

I've briefly highlighted some of the most common issues families experience when trying to confront grief. I think it's important to discuss these issues, because the more we understand why communication breaks down, the more we can learn to control our reaction in stressful situations.

Conflicting Memories of a Loved One

Are you surprised that Aunt Mildred remembers Grandmother differently from you? Do you find yourself getting upset every time Aunt Mildred complains that your grandmother wasn't an easy person to be around?

Often after a loved one passes away, surviving family get stuck in a tango of conflicting memories. One person feels hurt that the other doesn't remember the loved one in a favorable light. Conversely, a daughter might wonder why her brother never understood how hurtful Dad could be with his opinions. In extreme cases, surviving family members may discover a deep painful secret, like debt or an illicit affair, which paints their loved one in a negative light. Memory is as potent as emotions. We must learn to read and handle memory carefully, because it is a reflection of deeper issues within our psyche and soul.

• Solution: *Listen*

Aunt Mildred's grief and pain may seem more like anger and resentment, but try to remember that this is her form of grief. She needs your love and support more than ever. Listen, but refrain from commenting. Often people just want to be listened to and heard. They want a release from their anger and confusion. Try to feel empathy for her words and understand them independently of your memory. Try using validating words and phrases like, 'I sympathize with the way you're feeling right now.'

If you find Aunt Mildred is looking for a fight, listening and gentle words won't help. Create positive distance between you and an antagonizing family member. Send them love mentally and ask the angels to help you. If you are really finding it difficult to reach a positive compromise with a family member, ask the angels to help you cut the cord between you. There are plenty of books on this subject. However, be forewarned: this could result in a family member disappearing from your life. The angels take our prayers literally, so be very careful of your intention. It is important that you clarify what you would like to achieve long term with a family member, whether it is healing or permanent distance. Remember, distance rarely results in closure.

Inheritance

This is probably the biggest area for conflict in families. Things can often turn nasty when it comes to inheritance. A loved one's wishes in the will become distorted by old family feuds. History repeats itself and suddenly daughters are ready to kill each other over Mom's beloved slippers and robe. While real estate is commonly cited as a source of contention between siblings, it is the little things which threaten to sever relationships permanently.

I knew two sisters who didn't speak for three decades over their mother's slippers. This feud could be traced back to prior misunderstandings and old hurts, but it is such a shame they stopped talking to each other over something as silly as a pair of used white slippers. Admittedly, the slippers were handmade in France for their mother, but even this fact could not erase the arbitrariness of the feud. This story illustrates that conflicts over inheritance are a very real and painful reality after the loss of a loved one.

• **Solution:** *Compromise*

Compromise is never easy. If my cousins had been less stubborn, maybe they could have worked out an arrangement to share the slippers or exchange them in favor of something else like their mother's favorite hat. Their relationship was so strained that a pair of slippers broke down communication completely.

If one sister had recognized how much her sibling was suffering, perhaps things would have turned out differently. The relations would have softened and they might have been more willing to reach a positive compromise. Since neither sister showed compassion, this never happened. Compromise is commonly mistaken for being submissive. People want to appear strong and in control, especially during challenging times. This comes from the ego, not the heart. The need to be in control stems from fear of being out of control. If we pause to consider how others feel, we will find other ways to steel our strength, like sharing photos or memories of a loved one.

Different Ways of Expressing Grief

This is one of the biggest sources of tensions in families, especially between men and women. When my brother died, my mother couldn't understand why my father did not openly grieve for his son. It was a very confusing and hurtful time for her. Slowly, she learned about the different ways men and women express not only emotions, but also grief. Men tend to process their emotions externally, throwing themselves into projects or practical tasks. To a woman, it may seem like their partner is denying the significance of the loss. Conversely, the partner feels he is providing and protecting his family in the only way he knows how. Talking about feelings may make men feel uncomfortable, even emasculated. Women, on the other hand, have a very deep and real need to talk about their grief. Talking provides a much-needed outlet for internalized emotions.

Age also affects how people process and show grief. A very young child has not completely developed mentally and emotionally. Young children struggle to understand the impact of loss, whereas a teenager will most likely feel angry or hurt.

It is also important to note the very individual nature of grief. It manifests in people's lives in different ways. A highly emotional person will grieve in a very different way from a person who tends to be unemotional. There is no right way to grieve. Respect and compassion go a long way in bridging gaps in the different way people grieve.

• Solution: *Talk on Neutral Ground*

Men rarely feel comfortable in their homes talking about their feelings. This can make them feel vulnerable and emasculated. Try meeting on neutral ground, somewhere you can talk privately. A country lane or a quite coffee shop might offer the man in your life, whether it is your brother, father or partner, the perfect opportunity and setting to talk about the way he really feels.

Don't pressure him into speaking; remind him how much you care about him and that you are really interested to know how he is doing. If he clams up, talk about the way you feel. This might be enough to make the two of you feel better.

Some people might need more space to grieve than others. Whatever the age or background of a person, talking on neutral ground is essential. People are unlikely to open up in their everyday lives because of the individual pressures and anxieties they experience. If they are removed from these pressures, they are more likely to relax, listen and (with time) talk.

Why Families Are Instrumental in the Healing Process

Healing is a two-way street. We need to communicate our experiences and feelings with those closest to us in order to truly heal. Guidance comes in all forms, not just from the spiritual world but also in our everyday physical lives. What better place to get love and support than your family? Even if your family is not united or particularly close, the loss of a loved one presents a unique opportunity to heal and grow spiritually as a family.

Grief is a shared journey with many people. It is with this thinking in mind that I've written this book. I think families are instrumental in the healing process because they are the people who know you best. Even if your relationship isn't always harmonious, families can turn grief into a shared opportunity for guidance and growth. Think of the loss as one of the biggest tests you will face as a family. How would the person you have lost want you to behave? Most likely they would want you to be kind and generous to each other. They would want you to remember happy occasions together and celebrate their memory.

For there is no better memory than a life spent in the company of friends and family.

Conclusion

I was walking down an ancient cobbled street in Paris. I was 8 years old. It was Christmas Day. I will never forget the sight of the haggard old woman in the doorway of one of the buildings. She was a beggar, alone and crippled. She had two crutches and a head scarf. I felt empathy. How could a person be so alone? I was made afraid by the woman's isolation. It was a reminder that many people suffer in the world without relief or respite.

It was one thing to beg, but to beg at Christmas meant only one thing: she was desperate. It was Christmas Day; need I say more? Her cup was empty. Had no one noticed this woman on one of the most important holidays? This beggar was alone on a day when most people are surrounded by friends and family. I was with my family. *Where was her family?*

I immediately emptied the contents of my purse into her cup. My mother and father stopped walking. They watched the scene unfold, flabbergasted that their 8-year-old daughter had noticed the beggar and emptied her purse.

The woman wasn't a typical beggar. She didn't say 'Thank you.' Instead, she said, 'You are blessed by angels. Your life will be blessed by the angels and God.' She might have said this to every person who gave her money, but I sincerely doubt it. I have given money to many beggars; beggars I knew suffered from addictions and alcoholism. None has said my life would be blessed. They uttered kind words like, 'Thank you, God bless', but never such a stark declaration concerning my future.

When you think about it, it is not something someone begging for money would say. Usually people who find themselves in tough times do not think of the fortunes of others. Maybe she was moved by my youth. She was touched that a child felt intense compassion and empathy for her. I have no idea how long she had been sitting in the corner with her pitiful crutches, hunched over in the cold. I want to think she emptied the contents of her pockets every time someone gave her money. I refuse to believe that people can be so cruel and indifferent. Yet I know in my heart that she was ignored her whole life by many people, not just by strangers, but also by those closest to her. I felt it. I recognized her isolation. Real suffering cannot be faked. It is written in the face, eyes and posture. The woman had suffered her whole life.

I do not know why children are more capable of recognizing suffering than adults. I think as adults we develop thick skins. Suddenly, forgiveness and compassion become less of a focus. These feelings are replaced with judgment and conceit. We applaud entrepreneurs, but do we also recognize the importance of nurses and teachers in the same salutary manner? I think not. Too often nurses and teachers are thought of as downtrodden. People often say, 'Those who cannot do, teach.' I think this is an unfair assessment of one of the most important professions. I will be the first to admit that I owe a great deal of my success to my teachers, the ones who never stopped believing in me. The same is true of the many nurses I know. I don't want to imagine where I would be without their constant efforts.

I have spent a great deal of my life reflecting on what drives people. I am often shocked by the conversations I have with peers when they voice opinions about human nature or success. At times I feel naïve for building so much of my life on faith and spirituality, but I think the results speak for themselves. All too often we seek acceptance from others, when the answer lies within.

Grief versus Guidance

A part of me died the day my mother passed away. I will never again be that youthful, smiling girl I was before her death. You can see in the pictures before and after my mother's death the change that took place. It is clear the loss devastated me. Like every life-altering event, I found myself at a crossroad; not just one, but several. Every time I had to make a decision, I stumbled, stuttered and found excuses to avoid responsibility. For a very long time, I didn't want to grow up. The thought of being accountable for my actions was terrifying.

Grief paralyzed me. Grief does this to you. If you don't tackle it head on, it can stunt your growth. I made every effort to be positive and proactive in my life after Mom's death, but even that wasn't enough. I needed faith to heal my deepest wounds. Most of all I needed guidance.

Since losing my mother I have thought a lot about grief. I found that, much like faith, grief is elusive. People avoid discussing topics that creep into metaphysical territory. Friends and family are happy to discuss the weather, politics, economics and art, but when it comes to the tricky and often slippery area of human emotions they are quick to change the topic. Why is this? Surely, human emotions matter more than the weather. People think it is weak to speak about the way they feel, but I think it is a sign of strength. My experience has taught me that faith and grief are closely related. Faith and spirituality help us confront grief, and grief often unlocks the faith concealed in our heart. If we grieve for the loss of a loved one for a long time, it might be an indication that we need to steel our faith.

We are more connected than we like to believe. This is something Mom taught me in her messages. However, growing up, I felt differently. I never felt like I belonged. As a child I was quiet and retreating by nature. With friends, I often assumed the role of the jokester, making them laugh to release the inner pressure I felt to belong. In my teens and early twenties I would describe myself as an escapist. I was the quintessential misfit, rebelling in my teens and moving away when I was 15 to attend a school up north. I graduated and moved to London shortly after to attend university, where I met my husband and have lived ever since. Looking back on the last 10 years of my life, one thing is clear to me: I didn't know what I wanted to do with my life nor did I know the depths of my spirituality. I was constantly changing friendship circles, boyfriends and countries in a bid to find myself. Like many insecure people, I avoided standing out in the wrong ways. Unfortunately, this stunted my spiritual growth. I was unable to receive the guidance I so badly needed. I couldn't find a way to heal old wounds.

Mom was different. She didn't mind if people singled her out. Some of the best advice she ever gave me was: 'To thine own self be true.' She told me over and over that I didn't need to explain myself to people. This was a radical concept. All too often we come up with white lies to excuse our behavior, but most of us do not pause to wonder why we feel we need to explain ourselves to other people.

Once, when Mom decided I shouldn't attend an overnight school trip, the English teacher who organized the trip asked her, 'And what is your excuse?' as she leaned on our car; to which Mom curtly replied, 'I don't have to give you an excuse.' Ten seconds later, she rolled up the window and drove off without so much as uttering another word. Mom was famous for these kinds of scenes. Needless to say, my grades plummeted. I was lucky to pass the class after what Mom did.

I suppose this was a small price to pay in the grander scheme of things. This memory is etched in my childhood, immortalized in many late-night dinner anecdotes. Captive listeners usually ask, 'Did she really do that?' Yes, she *really* did that (I've got the grades to prove it) and I can't forget the moment. It is branded in my memory, much in the way a person stumbles across a stranger's name etched in a tree. That moment was Mom's calling card. Once I witnessed her defending her beliefs, I realized who my mother really was. My mother was a rash, abrupt person, but she was someone with honor and integrity. She followed her moral code until the end. Every child has this defining moment when they realize their parent is real, imperfect, yet utterly irreplaceable. Just a few years later I would understand how irreplaceable Mom really was.

It's true my life has been blessed by the angels, just as the woman predicted on the street so many years ago. Her stark words shocked my parents, but they sent a chill down my back. I knew that if I walked the line between faith and perseverance, I would be blessed with a rich, spiritual life to share with others.

I am also lucky enough to have a family that valued spirituality. I fondly remember my mother recounting stories of her family. Aunt Ethel was the most gregarious. She spent her days with a canary bird perched on her finger, working out in the morning nude on her exercise bike. For the record, she was alone when she exercised, but this didn't diminish her eccentricity. Incredibly, she drank a coke to begin her day.

Aunt Ethel could have inspired a Faulkner novel with all her Southern gothic mannerisms. She was originally from New York. At 68 she decided to move to the small town of Quincy, Florida to live out the last of her days with her sister-in-law. Aunt Ethel read continually. Most of her library was made up of spiritual works from the turn of the century like *The Impersonal Life* and *The Prophet*. Mom lovingly kept her books for many years, tucked away in a secret drawer. Now I am the proud owner of the well-thumbed early editions. Every time I read them, I feel Ethel's presence. She continues to inspire me.

Receiving Guidance

I hope my experience shows how instrumental spirituality is in our lives. Five years ago I made a promise to my mother to look for signs after she died. I kept this promise, but it hasn't always been easy. I was tempted to dismiss a lot of her messages as coincidences, but I knew in my heart they weren't coincidences. I tested Mom and she tested me. While she passed my tests, I can't say I always passed hers. I mentioned earlier that faith was a subject close to my heart and if there was a subject closer, it had to be skepticism. The temptation to ignore the evidence of Mom's presence in my life arose from the skeptic in me.

I didn't want to believe that Mom could make contact, because the thought hurt too much. There were so many things I had 'left undone.' I had the opportunity to make right my wrongs, but the pressure and weight of the responsibility was enormous. When people say, 'Let bygones be bygones', I think a lot of them are using death as an excuse not to take responsibility for their actions. However, if you could speak to your loved one whom you have lost, what would you say? Would you say, 'I am sorry' or 'I love you very much'?

Chances are, your loved one already knows how you feel. Imagine you could receive a sign from your loved one just so you knew he or she was okay. We are all capable of receiving guidance in the form of signs and messages. You may still find it difficult to believe, but pay attention closely and you will start to see the connections you previously missed or dismissed as coincidences. You will find, by being 'alert' or mindfully awake, that you are more prepared to receive guidance. The Parable of the Talents tells us, 'Be on the alert then, because you do not know the day nor the hour.' We can wait until the afterlife to see our loved ones or we can welcome them into our lives in the here and now with the help of angels. The decision is in your hands.

Reflections

I hope my story has inspired readers to explore their faith. There are so many questions about life and death which science fails to explain. I believe many of the answers to these questions lie within the deepest recesses of our consciousness. Bestselling books like *Heaven is for Real* by Todd Burpo or *Life after Life* by Raymond Moody explore the great mystery that still eludes us: What happens when you die? It is a simple enough question, but you would be surprised how many answers are found in an attempt to understand the complex working of the human body.

I think Todd Burpo's son's description of heaven is quite accurate. He describes it as a place of light, constant and infinite light. The idea of infinite light is an important concept which is central to this book. I explained in the opening chapters that the title, *A Circle of Light*, refers to light within us (the light of our soul) and the divine light outside of us. They are the same light.

Heaven is never dark, because the souls of the departed keep it alight. My mother appeared to me in a dream once. I don't dream of my mother often, almost never. I don't know if this is normal, but I rarely dream about people I know. I don't even dream about my husband. So I think it is more to do with me than my mother. When I do dream about her, it's because she has some kind of message to deliver. We rarely converse. She gives me the message and disappears as quickly as she appears. I often don't have time to react to the messages. I think this is to help me recognize the difference between a dream which is intended as guidance and a normal dream.

In one of the rare dreams when we spoke, I asked Mom what heaven looked like. She said she was surrounded by 'infinite beautiful, radiant light.' She also told me of God. I wish I could remember what she said. I think my brain purposely forgot because it's something I want to find out for myself. I had the dream before I started reading about the subject of life after death. I was struck by the similarity between my mother's account of heaven and Todd Burpo's son, Colton Burpo's description. I have read countless books about the afterlife, and all of them describe the same radiant light. The recurring imagery suggests there is some truth in these descriptions and in my mother's account.

They all share the same element, light. This theme is independent of religious ties. Like angels or elevated spiritual beings, light seems very much a universal theme common to many religions across the world and spiritual people. I was also stunned to read in another book that angels in heaven built a city in their mind whose walls sparkle like gold. The book stated that our loved ones wait for us and build houses together which might resemble the houses they loved and lived in while they were alive. On the other hand, these houses might resemble something fantastic of pure invention... like a modern house with big glass windows.

My breath grew shallow when I read this. Twenty-two years ago my mother and I discussed heaven while driving home from dance class. We spoke about my grandparents and baby brother who had passed away. Mom said they would live with us in heaven. We would build a big house with our imagination. I got carried away and immediately thought of a glass house. I thought we were playing a game, but Mom was much more serious. Especially when she told me she would go when it was her time.

From the earliest age, Mom was preparing me for the fact that we would not be together forever. She spoke about sending signs and how I might be able to keep contact with her. Her death was never a shock; it was devastating, but I always expected it. I didn't expect it to happen so soon, but I think she always knew she would die younger than most. Passing on at 58, there were a lot of things she didn't get to experience. I think that's why our communication, and the guidance which has come from it, has been so important for both of us. It helped heal many of the misunderstandings we had when I was a teenager. More importantly, it helped me overcome grief and use it as a positive tool in my life to give me a renewed sense of direction and purpose.

Mom is always around. If I ever doubted this fact, she has sent me signs (too many to count) to reassure me she is watching my life unfold. Our contact is not limited to signs; it has encompassed deeper messages that touch others' lives.

While we have not managed to prove there is an afterlife, I think numerous books, films and TV shows have broken the taboos that once surrounded the subject. People are more open to discussing their views in public. I am not sure we will ever be able to prove there is life after death. My proof is personal, just like my faith. I don't expect anyone to take my word as proof there is an afterlife. It's a question you need to ask yourself. The answers you find are yours and yours alone.

I can discuss my faith and the guidance which comes from it, but I can't show you how to open your heart to spirituality or receive guidance. Throughout the book I cite techniques, tools and exercises to help readers understand their unique journey to transform grief into guidance, but these are merely suggestions which I have found useful. Nor do I prescribe a particular religious view to accompany these techniques. My intention is not to sway readers, but to highlight my own views in an uplifting and educational way.

The suggested techniques, tools and techniques may not be useful or relevant to you. This is for you to decide. I treat each reader with loving respect and strongly believe readers will use their own prudence and sensibility before following these suggestions. In life, I believe it is important to take time to educate oneself on a subject before making a decision or involving others. The same is true of my book. I hope readers will read extensively on the subject of healing, grief, death and the afterlife. My book is one account of many. However, I think the candor and intimacy of my experience separates it from many works that are commercially motivated, and this is perhaps the best recommendation I can give for present and future readers.

Once again, I must also take the time to stress the fact that these techniques, tools and exercises are not and never have been a substitute for medical or psychological treatment. Readers follow the suggestions contained in this book at their own discretion and with their own judgment.

My father is a doctor, and I believe very strongly in established medical and psychological research and treatment. I am living proof of the reputability of the medical community. My life and wellbeing has been saved many times by medical professionals. So I urge any readers suffering from depression or any other ailment, whether psychological or physical, to seek out the advice and treatment of a regulated professional. There is no shame in seeking help to heal from deep-rooted pain. There is only strength.

My experience is simply an account of my journey to become more spiritual. At the start of my journey, I was very skeptical. Halfway through, I turned a new leaf and haven't looked back since. I finished the journey with a stronger sense of myself and my spirituality. This is all anyone can ask from an experience.

Whether you believe in an afterlife or not is another discussion. No one can deny the importance or the impact of a loved one on our life. Losing a loved one is next to losing a piece of you. How you fill the hole a loved one leaves is up to you. I welcomed my mother into my life. There is symmetry to my life, a shape and form which was previously missing. My hope is that you will find your own shape and form as unique as your individual purpose and every bit as special.

Light & Love,

Adele Vincent

About the Author

Adele Vincent realized there was a real need for an organization that promoted and discussed women's spirituality. This is how Ask Angel Women's Workshop came into being. Every woman can identify with the pressures of the 'have-it-all society.' Many women overlook their spirituality in the rat race to get to the top. By sharing her experiences with others, Adele learned that there were many women who have a powerful desire to discuss spirituality and form a deeper connection with their divine purpose.

Her book, *A Circle of Light: Transform Grief into a Unique Opportunity for Guidance*, and workshops provide readers with the tools to understand the importance of spirituality in our lives. She shows how each of us can find purpose in the journey to transform grief into guidance.